· 2 ·

Polyphony and Symphony in Prophetic Literature
Rereading Jeremiah 7–20

תורה נביאים כתובים
STUDIES IN OLD TESTAMENT INTERPRETATION

Series editors
Jeffrey S. Rogers, Furman University
Cecil P. Staton, Jr., Mercer University

1. *A Hermeneutic of Curiosity and Readings of Psalm 61* (1995)
2. *Polyphony and Symphony in Prophetic Literature.
   Rereading Jeremiah 7–20* (1996)

תורה נביאים כתובים

תורה נביאים כתובים

STUDIES IN OLD TESTAMENT INTERPRETATION

·2·

Polyphony and Symphony in Prophetic Literature Rereading Jeremiah 7–20

❑

Mark E. Biddle

❑

MERCER UNIVERSITY PRESS
·1996·

ISBN 0-86554-503-0

BS
1525.2
.B528
1996

MUP/H394

Library of Congress Cataloging-in-Publication Data

Biddle, Mark E.
Polyphony and symphony in prophetic literature :
rereading Jeremiah 7–20 / Mark E. Biddle.
x+136 pp. 6x9" (15x23cm.)—(Studies in O.T. interpretation ; 2)
Includes bibliographical references and index.
ISBN 0-86554-503-0 (hardcover : alk. paper)
1. Bible, O.T. Jeremiah vii-xx—Criticiam, interpretation, etc.
I. Title. II. Series.
BS1525.2.B528   1996
224'.206—dc20   96-3426

CIP

Contents

Dedication

to Hans-Harald Mallau
with gratitude

Preface

This study grows out of observations and issues I encountered while writing my dissertation on Jeremiah 2–3. In the intervening years I have felt myself drawn again and again to Jeremiah, an enigmatic book both *fascinans et trememdum* indeed.

Thanks are due to many people for their assistance. I have dedicated the book to Prof. Dr. Theol. Hans Mallau, my teacher and friend, now retired. His fascination with the Hebrew Bible and with the book of Jeremiah in particular have contributed immeasurably to my own.

Prof. Jeffrey Rogers has been a meticulous editor, a challenging colleague, and now a good friend. The library staff at Carson-Newman College have been very patient with my many interlibrary loan requests. Ms. George Anah Self merits special thanks. The manuscript was completed during a sabbatical leave from teaching responsibilities. I thank the trustees and administration of Carson-Newman for the privelege.

As always, my family—Lucia, Colin, and Graeme—have born a special burden when Dad is "Jeremiahing," as the boys put it. Colin is glad that, finally, I have finished this book.

Jefferson City, Tennessee
September 1995

Mark E. Biddle

Abbreviations

Abbreviations conform to the style cited in the *Society of Biblical Literature Membership Directory and Handbook 1994* (Atlanta: Scholars Press, 1994) and in the *Mercer Dictionary of the Bible* and the *Mercer Commentary on the Bible* (Macon GA: Mercer University Press, 1990 and 1995).

Introduction

Analysts and theorists in many disciplines have commented recently on the remarkable paradigm shifts observable in many fields of inquiry in this century. Newtonian mechanics has given way to wave-particle duality, quantum probability, and general relativity. In biology, the role of chance evolution is being challenged by understandings of life itself as the actualization of a pattern of self-organization. Commitments to the decidedly non-Enlightenment ideas of community and ecology, as opposed to individuality and manipulation, increasingly characterize contemporary social consciousness. Perceiving a relationship to an underlying *Zeitgeist*, some commentators have seen these developments in particular fields as evidence of a comprehensive paradigm shift, often termed "postmodernism."

The postmodern paradigm differs from modernism largely in relation to its theory of knowledge and its emphasis on holistic, systemic approaches. The new paradigm rejects modernism's objectivism and reductionism in favor of a Heisenbergian understanding of the process of knowing. According to this viewpoint, purely objective knowledge is simply unattainable since the knower participates in and inevitably influences the system under observation.[1]

A wide range of perspectives which may be loosely classified "postmodern" have also become prominent in biblical studies in recent decades. Feminist criticism, Marxist criticism, and reader-response criti-

---

[1]For discussions of the broader phenomenon see F. Capra, *The Tao of Physics*, 3rd ed. (Boston: Shambhala, 1991); id., *The Turning Point* (New York: Simon & Schuster, 1982); F. Capra, D. Steindl-Rast, and T. Matus, *Belonging to the Universe: Explorations on the Frontiers of Science and Spirituality* (San Francisco: Harper, 1991); W. Heisenberg, *Physics and Philosophy* (New York: Harper & Row, 1962); and T. Kuhn, *The Structure of Scientific Revolutions* (Chicago: University of Chicago Press, 1970).

cism, for example, share an understanding of language as a Heisenbergian system. The interpreter/reader construes texts in ways which yield meaning. These methods strenuously object to the positivistic, reductionistic, and atomistic tendencies of the modernist historical-critical methods of Biblical interpretation. They insist that the Biblical text be approached as a complete system (synchronically) instead of as a repository of historical data (diachronically).

How does one approach a system with the intention of comprehending holistically? Must one not begin somewhere? Several heralds of the new paradigm in the realm of science acknowledge the necessity of starting with some part of the system. As a result, these proponents of a new scientific paradigm do not call for the abandonment of "modern" scientific methods, since they provide the tools for examining the starting point, but for the utilization of these methods within the proper, holistic, framework for understanding the natural system. Scientists must study some manageable aspect of reality in order to gain insights which may improve the overall approximate understanding of reality as a whole.

The interrelated problems of a starting point, a method for detailed analysis, and a framework for understanding the entire system is familiar to biblical interpreters as the hermeneutical circle. The interpreter examines the several aspects of a text in detail in an effort to gain an approximate understanding of the whole. In a sense, the critical approaches associated with the historical-critical method may be considered tools for examining various aspects of the totality.[2] Calls for appreciation of the textual system as a whole appropriately recognize the limitations of historical criticism at this point. On the other hand, newer methods of biblical criticism fail to value equally all the particulars of the entire textual system as avenues toward understanding the whole. Scientific postmodernism recognizes that the system of nature is a complex unity subject to biological, chemical, geological, physical, and ecological analyses. The system may only be understood by considering all aspects together. Biblical scholarship has yet to acknowledge, similarly, that the goal of interpreting the final form of the text as a unit can only be achieved incrementally. Holistic understandings of textual systems can

---

[2]See, e.g., the approach of W. Bellinger, *A Hermeneutic of Curiosity and Readings of Psalm 61*, SOTI 1 (Macon GA: Mercer University Press, 1995).

only be approximated by the analysis of complex textual histories and structures.

Problem

The book of Jeremiah provides an opportunity to test the potential of such a holistic, systemic approach to the Bible. Jeremiah confronts the interpreter with the dual challenges of paying proper attention to its undeniable complexity and of coming, nevertheless, to some understanding of the whole. In particular, three issues which have long faced critical study of Jeremiah may be better understood when viewed from a systemic perspective as complementary. Each issue reflects the problem of the relationship of a particular aspect of Jeremiah to an understanding of the whole.

First, what is the structure of the book? Answers have included chronology, thematic arrangements, and blocks of tradition,[3] but little attention has been paid to factors which may have resulted from sophisticated literary (or redactional) activity.

Second, how does one account for the wide variety of styles, forms, and perspectives in the book? The classifications by B. Duhm[4] and S. Mowinckel[5] have dominated critical inquiry; but at least one of their categories, "A" material or "authentic" Jeremian poetry, has not been subject to analysis with rigor comparable to the other three categories. Critics usually work with source-critical (authentic/unauthentic; poetry is largely equated with authenticity) or form-critical categories (judgment/salvation/lament), assuming the oracular nature of prophecy. In fact, however, oracular forms constitute only a small proportion of materials in the poetry of Jeremiah 7–20. Much of this poetry represents the speech, not of the prophet or of God via the prophet, but of a variety of other figures expressing a wide range of sentiment and response to the crisis assumed by the book as a whole. Little attention has been paid to these other

---

[3]For an overview of positions concerning the structure of Jeremiah, see M. Biddle, *A Redaction History of Jeremiah 2:1-4:2*, AThANT 77 (Zürich: TVZ, 1990) 4-29.

[4]*Das Buch Jeremia*, KHC 11 (Tübingen: J.C.B. Mohr, 1901).

[5]*Zur Komposition des Buches Jeremia*, Videnskapsselskapets skrifter 4, Hist.-Filos. Klasse, 1913 no. 5 (Oslo: Kristiana, 1914).

voices, with the result that some features of the book produced by con-
scious literary or redactional activity have been overlooked.

Third, is it possible to arrive at an understanding of the genre of the
book of Jeremiah as a whole? Prevailing assessments of the book explain
its somewhat confusing structure as the result of the rather haphazard
collection of short units of various genre and from various original
settings. Such assessments do not appear to provide an adequate
framework for interpreting the interchange between the various figures
whose speech is represented in the text. A metageneric analysis of the
interplay between the shorter units in Jeremiah may contribute to a better
understanding of the relation of the short units to one another and to the
book as a whole.

Jeremiah 7–20 presents an opportunity to examine these three issues
as aspects of a single problem. Current critical opinion of Jeremiah 1–25
divides this first major poetical section of the book roughly into three
parts: Jeremiah 1–10 contains Jeremiah's "early" preaching warning
about the "enemy from the North";[6] Jeremiah 11–20 represents a group
of several blocks of material organized around a prose sermon/prophetic
confession/divine response pattern;[7] and Jeremiah 21–25 constitutes a
collection of oracles against the leadership. The current understanding of
Jeremiah 11–20 deserves particular attention because it overlooks the fact
that the pattern of prose/confession/response begins earlier than Jeremiah

---

[6]For an exemplary statement of this position, see R. Albertz, "Jer 2-6 und die
Frühzeitverkündigung Jeremias," *ZAW* 94 (1982): 20-47; see also K. Seybold,
Der Prophet Jeremia: Leben und Werk, Urban-Taschenbücher 416 (Stuttgart:
Kohlhammer, 1993); D. Böhler, "Geschlechterdifferenz und Landbesitz: Struktur-
untersuchungen zu Jer 2,2-4,2" in *Jeremia und die "deuteronomistische
Bewegung,"* ed. W. Gross, BBB 98 (Weinheim: Beltz Athenäum, 1995) 91-127;
and discussion below, 50-54, esp. nn. 7, 8.

[7]W. Thiel, *Die deuteronomistische Redaktion von Jeremia 1–25*, WMANT
41 (Neukirchen: Neukirchener, 1973) 287. Although subjected to significant criticism and modification, elements of Thiel's form-critical analysis have been influential on Jeremiah scholarship: cf., among others, K. O'Connor, *The Confessions
of Jeremiah: Their Interpretation and Role in Chapters 1–25*, SBLDS 94
(Atlanta: Scholars Press, 1988) 116-18, 156; M. Smith, *The Laments of Jeremiah
and Their Contexts: A Literary and Redactional Study of Jeremiah 11-20*,
SBLMS 42 (Atlanta: Scholars Press, 1990) 43.

11. In fact, Jeremiah 7–10 shares several features with the collections constitutive of 11–20, including a body of "lament" materials which function analogously to the confessions in 11–20. A preliminary examination of these "lament" materials reveals a complicated pattern of dialogue between various lamenters. In addition to Jeremiah's confessions, one finds divine monologues, communal confessions, and the distress cries of the personified city, Jerusalem.

These observations resurrect the three issues mentioned above: (1) What is the structure of Jeremiah 1–20? Where are its major divisions, and what are its controlling principles? More specifically, to what extent do the prophetic confessions of 11–20 truly control the structure of 1–20? Can a compositional model that recognizes strands of materials interwoven in a continuous fabric, instead of models dealing with blocks of tradition or chronologically or thematically arranged materials, enable the interpreter to discern patterns? (2) Can an interpretive stance attuned to the interplay of dialogue partners in the otherwise confusing amalgamation of forms, styles, and perspectives enable the interpreter to identify the contours of the discussion? (3) Can a more highly nuanced analysis of Jeremian poetry, an analysis attuned to literary (redactional) activity, reconfigure how investigators understand issues of genre, not only in Jeremiah 7–20, but also in the book as a whole and prophetic literature in general?

A New Approach

An interpretive method intended for the prophetic books of the Hebrew Bible must balance a number of concerns. It must reflect an awareness that an author may assume multiple voices. This awareness involves sensitivity to two common categories of error. On the one hand, the method must avoid the errors of synchronic readings which confuse "persona" with (implied) author. Both classical historical-critical and newer literary-critical approaches exhibit a methodological tendency to homogenize voices, to treat poetry somewhat one-dimensionally, and to overlook nuances of voice and characterization. Both are enchanted with the awareness that "Jeremiah," either the historical person or the literary personage, really or fictively, spoke/wrote the words contained in the book. As a consequence, they allow for no fully developed voices or distinct characters other than the prophet's. Source and form critics seemed satisfied with the identification of "A" material as an "authentic" source, while newer literary critics homogenize.[8] On the other hand, the method must avoid the oversights of diachronic methods which *automatically* equate multiple voices with multiple authors.

In addition to this increased sensitivity to characterization as a literary technique, the method must acknowledge that some voices in Jeremiah are so distinct that they must reflect distinct social and historical settings. The almost universal acknowledgement that prophetic books result from a long process of literary formation calls for greater awareness of voices whose distinction points to redactional origins. Diachronic methods have sought to link texts to specific historical situations. This enterprise, while worthwhile in its own right, meets with varying degrees of success owing to a number of factors. Any historical reconstruction is by nature speculative. Furthermore, the canonical process itself resulted in a generalization and universalization of the text which has made specific historical situations all the more difficult to discover. Newer hermeneutical theory calls attention, more basically, to the mimetic character of literature and undermines assumptions concerning the objective nature of linguistic reference. Nevertheless, authors or redactors cannot avoid reflecting the given social or historical setting in their work. The author's or redactor's dilemma, ideology, politics, or theology leaves its mark *on the text: it becomes a component of the*

---

[8]Difficulties associated with the failure to distinguish between various voices have surfaced most noticeably, perhaps, in scholarly attempts to assess the significance of first person speech in the book of Jeremiah. H. Reventlow (*Liturgie und prophetisches Ich bei Jeremia* [Gütersloh: Gerd Mohn, 1963]), a representative of form-critical excess, assumed the identification of the speaker of first person materials with the historical Jeremiah. As a result, he championed a highly problematical theory concerning the cultic intercessory role of the historical Jeremiah in particular, and of the prophets in general. T. Polk (*The Prophetic Persona: Jeremiah and the Language of the Self*, JSOTSup 32 [Sheffield: JSOT, 1984]), on the other hand, made a similar assumption on the literary level of "the prophetic persona," with surrealistic interpretive consequences. In Polk's view, the figure of Jeremiah somehow incorporates the perspectives and passions of both YHWH and the people into his own literary psyche. The "I" in Jeremiah represents the prophet *and* the people *and* YHWH in a confusion of layers and overtones. The recognition of distinct literary (and probably redactional) voices would have protected against these extremes.

characterization of the voice speaking in the text. Consequently, it is entirely valid for exegesis to employ historical-critical tools capable of analyzing this aspect of characterization and voicing.

Finally, the method must be capable of identifying each distinct voice, whether this distinction be on the synchronic or diachronic level of the literary formation of the text. For instance, it should be capable of distinguishing not only between Jeremiah and Jerusalem, but also between Jeremiah as spokesperson for the concerns of the Babylonian Golah and Jeremiah as spokesperson for those left in the land. Taken together, diachronic interests and synchronic concerns fueled by recent developments in hermeneutical theory require sensitivity to the presence of distinctive voices on two levels, the redactional and the dialogico-literary. An approach which respects the text, including its development, will seek to hear the text's various voices—whether speaking from different historical contexts or as a function of literary characterization—on their terms. Such an approach views the book of Jeremiah in its final form as the proceedings of an open forum. Through it one hears various Jeremiahs—the indignant prophet, the plaintive sufferer, the hopeful visionary. One hears various YHWHs, various incarnations of the people, various personifications of Jerusalem, and various incarnations of the postexilic worshipping community. They dialogue with one another on the pages of the book of Jeremiah. Without some method for discerning the distinctiveness of these voices, the reader risks hearing their dialogue as cacophony instead of the intricate polyphony intended at least by later stages of the redactional process. The method proposed here, which may be regarded as a variety of redaction criticism informed by literary and canonical concerns, seeks to avoid the deafness of newer methods toward the nuances in, for example, the voices of the various Jeremiahs portrayed in the book. These various Jeremiahs function as the prophetic spokespersons for various viewpoints. At the same time, the method seeks to avoid the deafness of conventional historical criticism toward the voices of characters within an otherwise "homogeneous" source layer.

In comparison to conventional historical methods, the method proposed here resembles the method employed by a geologist studying a metamorphic rock. Such a rock, formed over time by a process of sedimentation and subsequent thermal fusion, contains, in its current, solidified state, clues concerning its formation. Indeed, it presents the geologist with a permanently fixed image of its state at the time it solidified. The geologist studies its pattern of crystallization, stratification, and coloration, all with the awareness that the rock preserves what it was. Similarly, the interpreter of the book of Jeremiah confronts a final form which deserves to be interepreted as a unit, not as disjoint fragments of historical data; yet, many features of the final form itself require evaluation in terms of the composition and redaction history of the book. The discussion preserved in the final form of the book incorporates voices from several historical and social settings now fused into a whole.

In comparison to newer literary theory, the method proposed here resembles the task of the sophisticated concertgoer who hears not only the sound of the orchestra, but the voices of the different instruments and the various melodies, countermelodies, and harmonies contributing to the whole. The method to be employed here reflects an interest in developing something of a new harmonic theory of prophetic literature. Prior to the late Middle Ages only unison and octaves were considered "harmonic." Later composers began to employ fourths and fifths. The chief characteristic of Baroque music was counterpoint—several melodic lines moving somewhat independently yet harmoniously. Classical, Romantic, and Modern symphonic music came to encompass many instrumental voices, counterpoint, and fuller, richer harmonic structures, in a grand unity (not a grand unison).

Evidence highlighted by historical-critical methods suggests that prophetic literature more closely resembles symphonic music than plainsong. Historical methods tend to focus on the individual voices, while newer methods focus impressionistically on the harmony of the whole. Prophetic music is symphonically complex, yet no approach currently in use views the prophets symphonically. Each in their own way, both historical-critical and literary readers of prophetic symphony have ears trained only to hear plainsong.

Method

Three basic questions will govern analysis of the symphony of voices in the book of Jeremiah. At a *first* level, it will be necessary to delimit the boundaries of speech. This most immediate concern involves the basic, text-imminent identification of speakers, addressees, and referents: From the text's perspective, who speaks? To whom? About whom or what? Jeremiah scholarship often falters at this most basic level of analysis due to a failure to allow the text full authority and integrity. An example, which will be treated in greater detail below, illustrates the importance of clarity on this issue. In a series of texts in Jeremiah an individual feminine character speaks, is spoken to, or is spoken about. Several texts identify this sometimes anonymous character as Jerusalem/Zion. Despite the text's clear intention to personify the capital city, interpreters of the book regularly treat her as if she were synonymous with collective portrayals of the people. Such interpretations overlook the ideological implications of the capital city personified as mother and queen in the society of other personified leading cities of the world. Just as the Statue of Liberty, Lady Liberty, does not represent a personification of the American people, but of the political principles which Americans hold dear, Lady Zion personifies a concept.

The *second* level of analysis involves the characterization of the figure identified. Once major figures have been identified in a given passage, it remains to attend to the text's portrayal of the *nature* or *character* of these figures. Not only do interpreters fail to hear the distinctive voice of Lady Zion owing to inadequately nuanced methods, for example, they also regularly force the text to conform to certain theological presuppositions such as those concerning the nature of God and the prophetic office. For example, several lament texts in Jeremiah 7–10 seem prima faciae to be God's statements of sorrow over his wayward people and the punishment they face. Often the oracular formulae, "Thus says YHWH" and "utterance of YHWH," explicitly mark these texts as divine speech. Yet many scholars emend or interpret them in ways which mitigate the distasteful element of divine pain. Despite the text's attribution of this speech to the deity, scholars regularly assign it to the prophet.

The *third* level pertains to the structure of the dialogue between these figures. Armed with observations on the level of the identity and character of the individual voices in the book, an interpretation of the contours, shapes, and dynamics of the dialogue which comprises the whole may be undertaken. The vitality, nuance, and force of the symphony can be expected to emerge most clearly when each voice is heard in proper balance and clarity.

Seven basic criteria serve the goals of this method. Three reflect the primary interest in delimiting the *identity* of major voices in a text, three concern data required for a full *characterization*, and the final criterion focuses upon the contours and shape of the *dialogue* as a whole.

Identity

Three criteria are concerned with identifying speakers, addressees, and referents. First, attention is given to grammatical and syntactical indicators of the identities of major figures, the contours of the dialogue between figures, and the extent of the current scheme. Older source criticism tended to utilize this data almost mechanistically—"The shift in speaker/number/gender in v 5 marks the beginning of a new unit." The method employed here is interested also in the identity and integrity of the figure indicated. While more recent methods have overlooked the significance of such variations, the present method will emphasize the integrity of individual voices. Second, structural elements such as chiasm, inclusio, and versification, among others, may point to the presence of competing schemes and call attention to dialogue between figures. It should be stressed that the method intends to be attuned to intervoice dialogue on either the synchronic or diachronic level. Third, tensions of theme, viewpoint, presupposition, and so forth, can confirm the presence of distinct voices. This criterion also suggests the need to consider the possibility that a given figure may speak with several distinct voices.

Characterization

Three criteria enable the investigator to develop a more complete understanding of individual figures and of the extended dialogue which provides the structure of the book. In contrast to the primarily denotative criteria discussed above, these criteria focus on connotation, nuance, and characterization. First, stylistic, thematic, ideological, traditional, and conceptual similarities can define a family of texts in the same voice. Second, using these families of texts, questions other than the mere identification of the voice can explored. The full implications of any characterization will not be exhausted solely through denotative avenues. Who, specifically, is "Israel" in a given text or family of texts? Northerners? Southerners? Exiles? Postexilic inhabitants of the land? What is this "Israel" like? Sinful? Repentant? Angry? Divided? United? Who speaks of "Israel" in this particular fashion? The privileged? The excluded? Those in exile? Those left in the land? Third, attention will be paid to the positions articulated by voices assuming the same basic identity in an effort to discriminate nuances of characterization, sociohistorical contexts presupposed, and positions represented.

Dialogue

Finally, by analyzing the interplay of the various voices in the book across a major block of the text, it may be possible to discover the contours of an extended dialogue and to shed light on questions of the structure, composition, and argument of the book of Jeremiah. The autonomy, integrity, and interrelatedness of these divergent voices must be preserved in interpretation, due not only to concern for literary theory, but also out of respect for the process of formation and the canonical status of the final product. The canonical text has captured voices in perpetual dialogue. This dialogue must be heard on its terms.

The method proposed here considers it important not to dissolve, or even resolve, but to recognize tensions and distinctives. The result will be an analytical matrix along three axes: (a) the basic identity of voices, (b) a characterization of individual voices involving both synchronic description and an analysis of the social and historical context against which these voices may best be heard, and (c) a description of the dialogue which reflects the richness of the individual voices (both in terms of characterization and historical setting) *and* the symphonic effect of the whole.

Plan

This study will examine three dialogical matrices in Jeremiah 7–20 in an effort both to test and refine the method outlined above and, of course, to shed light on a very complex unit of prophetic literature. As indicated above, the book of Jeremiah, especially Jeremiah 7–20, provides a potentially rich specimen of polyphonic prophetic dialogue. In some cases, voices dominant in Jeremiah 7–20 can also be heard in other portions of the book, or they dialogue with voices heard elsewhere. Such materials outside Jeremiah 7–20 will also be adduced to supplement the characterization of these voices or the analysis of these dialogues. Voices will be identified, characterized, and analyzed as constituents of multi-party dialogue.

This study will not, however, attempt an exhaustive reading of every voice and dialogue in Jeremiah 7–20. Space will permit only the treatment of a few test cases. The three dialogues to be examined have been chosen because the typical prophetic voice expressed in oracles of judgement and salvation does not enter into these discussions. A chapter will be devoted to each of the three dialogue matrices discernible in Jeremiah 7–20: (1) God, people, and city all lament Judah's fate; (2) God and the petulant prophet debate the proper role of prophetic intercession; and (3) God and the worshipping community debate the proper understanding of pardon and forgiveness, especially in relation to the status of the chosen nation in relation to its neighbors. Following the identification and characterization of the participants in these dialogues, a concluding chapter will offer a description of the structure of the larger system (Jeremiah 7–20) and will suggest implications for the interpretation of Jeremiah and prophetic literature in general.

Before proceeding with the study proper, it is appropriate to comment further[9] on the justification for treating Jeremiah 7– 20 as a major subsection of the book of Jeremiah. In fact, the decision to include Jeremiah 7–10 already reflects the concerns of the method proposed above.

M. Smith, who representatively argues for the subdivision of Jeremiah 11–20 into four parts (11–12, 13–15, 16–17, 18–20), notes five characteristics shared by his four confession complexes.[10] Each begins with a superscription followed by Deuteronomistic prose narrating a sermon or a symbolic act. Each prose narrative begins with two commands. Finally, if the endings of the first, third, and fourth sections are secondary, as Smith thinks, each section ends with a confession.[11]

Smith does not observe, however, that Jeremiah 7–10 also exhibit this pattern. Jeremiah 7–10 offer the first instance of the superscription, "the word which came to Jeremiah from the Lord," the standard form in subsequent passages.[12] Similarly, Jeremiah 7:1 introduces an extensive unit of Deuteronomistic prose, the first major prose sermon in the book. The narrative begins with the dual command to "stand in the gate and proclaim there this word." Jeremiah 7–10 does not end with a confession, but includes a significant concentration of lament materials (including

---

[9]See above, 6.

[10]*Laments*, 43.

[11]*Laments*, 38-40.

[12]Smith intentionally disregards a hypothetical earlier form of the superscription to the entire book, Jer 1:1. He also sets aside the superscription in Jer 3:6. It appears in the form, "and YHWH said to me," indicating a degree of continuity with the context, not a new beginning as does the asyndetic form in Jer 7:1.

calls to lament and repudiations of lament) whose relationship to later confessions will be explored in greater detail below.

Furthermore, Smith does not note that, as the prose in the confession collections, the Temple Sermon in Jeremiah 7 focuses on the common JerD themes of the people's failure to heed YHWH's word (Jer 7:21-28; compare 11:6-8; 13:10-11; 16:12; 18:10; 19:15) and their idolatry (7:30-34; cf. 11:9-13; 13:10-11; 16:11-13; 19:4-5,13).[13] Finally, YHWH's repeated prohibition against prophetic intercession first appears in Jer 7:16-20 (compare 11:14; 14:11-12; 16:5-9).

Jeremiah 7–10 share several features with Jeremiah 11–20, then, and can best be considered an integral segment of the larger unit Jeremiah 7–20. More precisely, Jeremiah 7–10 may best be characterized as a bridge unit linking Jeremiah 2–6 and 11–20. Several observations and lines of argument, developed below, will support this thesis.

---

[13]For concise treatments of the theology of the Deuteronomistic school, see esp. O. H. Steck, *Israel und das gewaltsame Geschick der Propheten: Untersuchungen zur Überlieferung des deuteronomistischen Geschichtsbildes im Alten Testament, Spätjudentum und Urchristentum*, WMANT 23 (Neukirchen: Neukirchener, 1967) 67, 138; and E. Nicholson, *Preaching to the Exiles: A Study of the Prose Tradition in the Book of Jeremiah* (Oxford: Basil Blackwell, 1970).

"Non-Oracular" Lament Materials in Jeremiah 7–20: God, People, and City in Dialogue[*]

Jeremiah traditionally has been described as the "weeping prophet" because of the high concentration of lament and confessional materials in Jeremiah 1–20. A special subcategory of these laments, the so-called "confessions," has attracted considerable scholarly attention over the years because of its apparently private, very plaintive, almost petulant character. Until recently, scholars usually regarded these confessions as somewhat unique intimations of the conflicted "inner life" of a major prophet. Similarly, the other first person laments in Jeremiah 1–20 have regularly been seen as confirmation of Jeremiah's sensitivity.[1]

This picture of the romantic prophet no longer enjoys universal acceptance. Because of the similarities between the confessions and certain of the Psalms of individual lament, some scholars have suggested that the presence and placement of the confessions may be attributable to redactional efforts to portray Jeremiah as the paradigmatic righteous sufferer. Others have voiced concerns about the dangers inherent in psychoanalyzing long-dead prophets on the basis of a written text, itself probably a composite work. Still others have argued that questions of authenticity and psychology should be abandoned in favor of analysis of

---

[*]Portions of this chapter were read in the Formation of the Book of Jeremiah Consultation at the 1993 SBL Annual Meeting, Washington, D.C., under the title "Confessional Materials in Jeremiah 7–10."

[1]See, as examples of an older generation of scholarship, W. Baumgartner, *Die Klagegedichte des Jeremia* (Giessen: Alfred Töpelmann, 1917); J. Skinner, *Prophecy & Religion: Studies in the Life of Jeremiah* (Cambridge: University Press, 1922) 201-30; and, S. Blank, *Jeremiah: Man and Prophet* (Cincinatti: Hebrew Union College Press, 1961) 105-28.

the structure and function of the confessions within the book of Jeremiah, as a whole.[2]

The problem of the structure and function of the lament materials in Jeremiah 1–20 seems well-suited, then, to the method outlined above. Taking the individual passages which comprise the larger lament category, can speakers be more precisely identified, characterized, and interpreted as voices in dialogue? Will such an analysis support the commonly held image of (the historical or literary) Jeremiah as the sensitive prophet par excellence? Do the confessions, in fact, play the dominant role often ascribed to them? Do the laments of Jeremiah 7–10

---

[2]For a summary of scholarship representative of the transition from the concerns of the older generation to newer viewpoints, see D. Jobling, "The Quest of the Historical Jeremiah: Hermeneutical Implications of Recent Literature," in *A Prophet to the Nations: Essays in Jeremiah Studies*, L. Perdue and B. Kovacs, eds. (Winona Lake: Eisenbrauns, 1984) 285-97 (= *Union Seminary Quarterly Review* 34 [1978]: 3-12). The following works have figured prominently in the new discussion concerning the interpretation of Jeremiah's confessions: Reventlow, *Liturgie*; E. Gerstenberger, "Jeremiah's Complaints: Observations of Jer. 15:10-21," *JBL* 82 (1963): 393-408; J. Bright, "Jeremiah's Complaints: Liturgy, or Expressions of Personal Distress?" in *Proclamation and Presence: Old Testament Essays in Honor of Gwynne Henton Davies*, ed. J. Durham and J. Porter (London: SCM, 1970) 189-214; A. Gunneweg, "Konfession oder Interpretation im Jeremiabuch," *ZTK* 67 (1970): 395-416; F. Hubmann, *Untersuchungen zu de Konfessionen: Jer 11:18–12:6 und Jer 15:10-21*, FB 30 (Echter: Echter, 1978); N. Ittmann, *Die Konfessionen Jeremias: Ihre Bedeutung für die Verkündigung des Propheten* (Neukirchen-Vluyn: Neukirchener, 1981); F. Ahuis, *Der Klagende Gerichtsprophet: Studien zur Klage in der Überlieferung von der altestamentlichen Gerichtspropheten* (Stuttgart: Calwer, 1982); T. Polk, *Prophetic Persona*; A. R. Diamond, *The Confessions of Jeremiah in Context: Scenes of Prophetic Drama*, JSOTSup 45 (Sheffield: JSOT Press, 1987); K. O'Connor, *The Confessions of Jeremiah: Their Interpretation and Role in Chapters 1–25*, SBLDS 94 (Atlanta: Scholars, 1988); K. Pohlmann, *Die Ferne Gottes—Studien zum Jeremiabuch: Beiträge zu den "Konfessionen" im Jeremiabuch und ein Versuch zur Frage nach den Anfängen der Jeremiatradition*, BZAW 179 (New York: Walter de Gruyter, 1989); M. Smith, *Laments*; D. Bak, *Klagender Gott—klagende Menschen: Studien zur Klage im Jeremiabuch*, BZAW 193 (New York: Walter de Gruyter, 1990).

resemble the prophetic confessions in placement or function? Do the laments uniformly reflect the sensitivities of the individual prophet?

Voices in Dialogue

In terms of the three basic criteria suggested above, examination of these laments suggests the following. First, in terms of the basic identification of voices, lament/confessional material in Jeremiah 1–20 falls into four major categories according to speaker and function: (1) spontaneous emotional responses to disaster voiced either by the community or by personified Lady Zion (including both laments and calls to lament), (2) communal confessions of guilt, (3) divine monologues, and (4) prophetic confessions. Notably, several texts usually regarded as expressions of Jeremiah's anguish seem rather to be statements of the community or the deity, and the prophet occupies a central role only in the individual confessions in Jeremiah 11–20. Secondly, each of these four speakers represents clearly distinct positions, characterized by particular attitudes and viewpoints regarding Judah's predicament. The community expresses either dismay or contrition. The prophet seems preoccupied with his own vindication. Only God voices any awareness of the ambiguity and conflict involved in the punishment of the chosen people. In comparison with the other voices in this dialogue, God appears to be the complex, "human," sensitive character. Finally, the contexts of several of these passages confirm the propriety of a dialogical model for interpreting laments in Jeremiah. In many instances, the prophetic oracle, the expected genre of prophetic discourse, plays little or no role in the dialogue.

Voices in Jeremiah 4:3-31: A Community in Crisis

Jeremiah 4:3-31 offers a particularly instructive illustration of the manner in which careful attention to the standard criterion of speaker can clarify the function of the laments and calls to lament which comprise the first category. In this extended passage, the prophetic persona gives way to the voices of the dramatis personae in dialogue. In it, the voices of the community, its representative, Lady Zion, and its God interact without the benefit of prophetic mediation or moderation.

The Community. Jer 4:3 continues a dialogue between God and the people of Judah. Except for Jer 4:1-2,[3] 4:9-10, and 4:23-26, God speaks directly to the people or to personified Jerusalem who respond spontaneously to catastrophe threatened or experienced.

[3]For thus says YHWH to the men of Judah and to Jerusalem:

"Plow your new ground
    and do not sow among thorns.
[4]Circumcise yourselves to YHWH
    and remove the foreskins of your hearts,
        men of Judah and inhabitants of Jerusalem,
Or my wrath with break out like fire
    and burn with no one to extinguish it
        because of your evil deeds.

[5]Announce in Judah and in Jerusalem proclaim and say:
'Sound the horn in the land!' Cry aloud and say:[4]

    'Assemble and let us flee
    to the fortified cities!'

[6]Raise a signal toward Zion!
    Flee! Do not stand around!
For I bring evil from the North
    and great destruction.
[7]A lion has gone up from its thicket
    and a destoyer of nations has set out;
He has left his place

---

[3]See M. Biddle, *Redaction*, 115, 165.

[4]The prosody of this introduction is ambiguous. Either the two tripartite formulae stand in a parallel relationship (cf. Jer 46:14; 50:2: Isa 48:20), the understanding reflected in the translation above, or the second introduction is itself part of the statement to be "announced in Judah and proclaimed in Jerusalem" (cf. Hos 5:8). In the latter case, the text records YHWH's instruction to the prophet to instruct his hearers to raise the cry of alarm. Although the resolution of this question does not represent a crucial issue for the current study, the fact that v 5 at least begins as YHWH speech and v 6 resumes YHWH speech suggests the simpler solution. Only v 5b is cited speech.

to make your land a ruin.

[8]Because of this, don sackcloth, lament, and wail:

'The burning wrath of YHWH has not turned from us'."

. . . .

[13]"Look! Like clouds he rises,
    like the whirlwind his horses,
swifter than eagles his horses—
    Woe to us, we are destroyed!"

Plural imperatives, second person plural possessive pronouns, and the phrase "my wrath" mark Jer 4:3-4 as divine direct address to the community. Jer 4:5-8 continues with plural imperatives and divine self-references, "I am bringing evil." The people's statements in 4:5c and 8b are as envisioned or prescribed by God.[5] The spontaneous emotional response to disaster in its most direct form first occurs in Jer 4:13. Within the context of Jeremiah 4, this exclamation constitutes the first statement of the community not suggested to the people by God.[6]

---

[5]W. McKane (*A Critical and Exegetical Commentary on Jeremiah*. Vol. 1. *Introduction and Commentary on Jeremiah I–XXV*, ICC [Edinburgh: T.&.T. Clark, 1986] 90) typifies a variety of scholarship unable to overcome the awareness that the prophet or the curators of his tradition spoke or penned the words recorded in the book of Jeremiah. He takes Jer 4:5 to be God's address to the prophet *despite the plural imperative verbs*. Why would God speak to Jeremiah in such a way? The dynamics of the book of Jeremiah require that the reader maintain a clear distinction between the literary characters, e.g., the participants in the literary dialogue, and the *historical* characters who recorded/composed the dialogue.

[6]Cf. R. Carroll, *Jeremiah: A Commentary*, OTL (London: SCM, 1986) 164. Again, McKane's interpretation (*Jeremiah*, 97-98) stumbles over an awareness of "reality": "Since Yahweh is not the speaker in v. 13 . . . and since vv 14-15 are, probably, spoken by Jeremiah rather than by Yahweh, it would then be possible to maintain that vv 11-15 . . . are words of Jeremiah and not of Yahweh."

Lady Zion. Jer 4:14-18 shifts the focus from the dialogue between God and the people—although echoes remain (4:15-16)—to the interchange between God and Lady Jerusalem.

> [14]"Wash wickedness from your heart, O Jerusalem,
>   so that I may save.
> How long will you harbor in your heart
>   wicked thoughts?"
>
> [15]A voice announces from Dan,
>   and proclaims disaster from Mount Ephraim:
>
> [16]"Tell the nations, 'Look!'
> Declare to Jerusalem:
>   'Besiegers come from a distant land,
>   they raise their voices against Judah's cities.
> [17]Like guardians of a field they surround her,
>   because she has rebelled against me,'
>   says YHWH,
> [18]'Your ways and your deeds
>   have done this to you,
> This is your evil,
>   it is bitter,
>   it has reached your heart'."
>
> [19]"My stomach! My stomach! I writhe!
>   The walls of my heart! I cannot be silent!
> For my soul hears the sound of the trumpet,
>   the alarm of war.
> [20]Crash after crash is heard,
>   for the whole land is destroyed.
> Suddenly my tents are destroyed,
>   in a moment my curtains.
> [21]How long must I see the signal,
>   hear the sound of the trumpet?"

In the previous section, God's warnings and threats in vv 3-12 elicit the people's frightened response in v 13. Does God's appeal to Lady Jerusalem in v 14 also elicit an emotional response?

Scholars often consider Jer 4:19-21 an example of Jeremiah's emotional involvement with and empathy for his people.[7] K. Kumaki argues persuasively, however, that plural references to "my tents" and "my curtains" indicate that Jerusalem speaks here, not Jeremiah. He points out that these expressions, including the reference to "my cords" in the parallel Jer 10:20 (compare Isa 54:2-3) have affinities with Jerusalem traditions.[8] In his view, the "Woe is me" cry of Jerusalem in 4:31 echoes the cry of 4:19.[9] God's appeal to Lady Jerusalem evokes a response similar to the people's frightened response to God's warnings in Jer 4:3-13.

Several other arguments support Kumaki's contention. The speaker in the parallel Jer 10:20 refers to "my children." The language of 4:19—"writing" (אוֹחִילָה; compare 4:31 כְּחוֹלָה, "like a woman in childbirth"), "my bowels"—suggests the image of a woman in childbirth, a common metaphor for personified Jerusalem.[10] In Jer 4:30 God addresses Zion as the "destroyed One" (שָׁדוּד), an apparent allusion to Zion's desperate response in 4:20 (שֻׁדְּדוּ). Both Jer 4:19-22 and 4:30-31 employ נֶפֶשׁ idiomatically for "self, I, me" (4:19 "נַפְשִׁי hears"; 4:31 "נַפְשִׁי faints"; compare 15:9).[11]

---

[7]Cf. F. K. Kumaki, "A New Look at Jer 4,19-22 and 10,19-21," AJBI 8 (1982): 113-14 for a summary of scholarly interpretations.

[8]F. Kumaki ("New Look," 115-16) prefers to refer to a tabernacle tradition.

[9]F. Kumaki, "New Look," 113, 116.

[10]See M. Biddle, "Lady Zion's Alter Egos: Isaiah 47:1-15 and 57:6-13 as Structural Counterparts," in *New Visions of the Book of Isaiah*, ed. R. Melugin and M. Sweeney, JSOTSup (Sheffield: JSOT, forthcoming); cf. Carroll, *Jeremiah*, 167.

[11]Although aware of the prominence of the Lady Jerusalem figure in Jer 4:19-22, e.g., T. Polk (*Persona*, 69) prefers to hear Jeremiah in, through, or behind Jerusalem's statement: "when [Jeremiah] speaks of "the walls of my heart" in 4.19 and employs the tent imagery in v 20, it is not too fanciful that we should hear Jerusalem's voice resonating in his own or that his persona has, as it were, blended into and fused with the persona of Jerusalem." Polk's thesis seems to be that, since the tradition identifies the prophet Jeremiah as the immediate human agent of all the speech contained in the book, every first person language specimen involves, to some degree or on some level, the prophetic persona. Can the integrity of distinct voices survive such an interpretive

Jeremiah 4:30-31 refers to and quotes Lady Jerusalem although the speaker is not immediately clear.

^{30}And you, Destroyed, what are you doing?
    You dress in crimson, accessorize with gold jewels,
You highlight your eyes with cosmetics,
    Futilely you beautify yourself:
Your lovers reject you;
    They seek your life.

^{31}I hear a voice like a woman in labor,
    Pain like a woman giving birth to her firstborn.
The sound of the daughter Zion gasping to breathe,
    Reaching out with her hands.

"Woe is me! I am fainting!
    My life is for the killers."

Following the haunting first-person visionary account in vv 23-26, God pronounces the reason for the cataclysm: "for I have spoken" (v 28). The speaker of vv 29-31 describes the abandonment of towns in Judah, reproaches Jerusalem directly, and reports hearing Jerusalem's anguished cry. Given the authoritative tone of the reproach and the absence of any indication of a change of speaker following v 28, no compelling reason for denying vv 29-31 to God presents itself. At any rate, even if this passage should be assigned to the prophet, it offers no insights into the emotional status of the speaker. Instead, it represents another example of the dialogue technique employed throughout Jeremiah 4: sudden shifts of speaker, real and fictive, without explicit markers.[12]

With the exceptions, then, of the prose comment on false prophets in 4:9-10 and the eery vision report in 4:23-26 (neither expresses mourning, complaint, or confession) Jeremiah 4 can be read as a dialogue between God, the people, and Jerusalem. Jeremiah 4 does not portray a prophet participating in his people's sorrow and anguish.

---

program?
    [12]W. McKane (*Jeremiah*, 111-13) and P. Craigie (Craigie, et al., *Jeremiah 1–25*, WBC 26 [Dallas: Word, 1991] 84) interpret this passage with an awareness of this technique, although they overlook it in other passages in Jeremiah 4–6.

Voices of the Community in Crisis outside Jeremiah 4

Other lament texts in Jeremiah 4–6 exhibit similar characteristics. Jeremiah 6:4-5 presents a particularly interesting case of unmarked dialogue, apparently between Jerusalem's attackers and her inhabitants:

"Prepare to attack her! Rise, let us go up at noon!"

"Woe to us, for the day turns, night comes!"

"Rise! Let us go up against her by night
and destroy her fortifications!"

Despite the total absence of indicators and the standard understanding of this exchange as a dialogue within the ranks of the attacking army,[13] the cry of woe in 6:4b seems best suited to the defenders of the city.[14] The people express simple, yet profound terror.

Even Jer 6:26, often interpreted as Jeremiah's personal statement ("my people"/"us"), conforms to the pattern established in Jeremiah 4. BHS follows the Leningrad Codex in failing to recognize the poetical structure of this unit. The text scans as seven lines, usually of four beats. It may be divided into four sections.

[24]"We hear news of it / our hands fall.
Distress grips us/ pain like childbirth."

[25]Do not go into the field / in the path do not walk,
     because of the enemy's sword / terror all around.
[26]Daughter of my people, don sackcloth / roll in ashes,
     mourn as for an only child, / bitter lamentation:
"Suddenly comes/ the destroyer upon us."

---

[13]W. Rudolph, *Jeremia*, HAT 1/12 (Tübingen: J.C.B. Mohr, 1947, [3]1967) 36; J. Thompson, *The Book of Jeremiah*, NICOT (Grand Rapids, Michigan: Eerdmans, 1980) 254; McKane, *Jeremiah*, 138. Carroll (*Jeremiah*, 192) recognizes the possibility of a dialogue between attackers and defenders but takes no definite position.

[14]With W. Holladay, *Jeremiah 1: A Commentary on the Book of the Prophet Jeremiah Chapters 1–25*, Hermeneia (Philadelphia: Fortress, 1986) 206: "The enemy might have said 'It's hopeless!' . . . but hardly 'Woe to us!'."

The chiastic structure of this unit and the shift from plural to second feminine singular verb forms suggest that the people express their anguish in 6:24 and 6:26c, while prohibitions and injunctions addressed to Zion comprise 6:25 and 6:26a,b. The recitative, not causal, כִּי in 26b (following the *verbum dicendi* אָבֵל) introduces the lament.

This use of כִּי to indicate the structure of dialogue is somewhat characteristic of Jeremiah 7–20. Jer 4:8, 7:29, and 9:16-21(English, 17-22) offer parallel constructions. Yahweh announces that he is bringing destruction upon Jerusalem (4:6b-7) and suggests that the people grieve and mourn. His suggestion includes a proposed *qinah*.

> Because of this don sackcloth / lament and wail: (כִּי)
> "The fierce anger of YHWH has not turned away from us."   (Jer 4:8)

Yahweh instructs personified Lady Zion to voice the *qinah* fragment in Jer 7:29b:

> Cut your hair and discard it /
> raise a lament on the bare heights: (כִּי)
>
> "YHWH rejects and forsakes /
> the generation of his wrath."

Lady Zion is to refer to the people in the third person as "the generation of his wrath." Such references which distinguish clearly between Lady Jerusalem and the people, her children, are relatively common in and outside Jeremiah (Isa 49:20; 51:18,20; 60:4). They call attention to the narrative distinction between the Zion figure and the more prosaic image of the people as a collective entity.

The complex dialogue involving YHWH, the people, and professional mourners in Jer 9:16-21(English, 17-22) offers another pointed example. This intricate, multilayered system of citations, demands careful attention.

> 16(17)Thus says YHWH Sebaoth:
>
> "Consider and call / for the wailers and let them come.
> Send for the skilled / and let them come.
> 17(18)Let them hurry / and raise laments over us.
> And let our eyes flow with tears /
> and our eyelids drip with water."

18(19)Yea (כִּי), a lament is heard in Zion:

"How we are destroyed/ greatly ashamed!
For we have abandoned our land /
     we have been thrown out of our homes."

19(20)(כִּי) Hear, O Women, the word of YHWH /
Give ear to the word of his mouth:

"Teach your daughters laments /
     Every one teach her friend mourning songs: (כִּי)

20(21)'Death has climbed into our windows /
     entered our strongholds,
cutting off children from the streets /
     youths from the squares.' "15

21(22)He speaks! Thus says YHWH:

"Corpses fall to the ground /
     like dung on the surface of the field
and like sheaves behind the reapers /
     and none to gather."

First YHWH counsels the people, presumably, to call for professional mourners so that the grave situation confronting Judah may be properly lamented. Indeed, a voice from Zion decries the destruction and abandonment which has befallen Judah. Once again YHWH counsels the wom-

---

15T. Polk's (*Persona*, 46, esp. n. 26) interpretation that Jeremiah identifies himself with the people here depends upon his assumption that the literary persona "Jeremiah" intermeshes with all other literary personae in the book. Linguistically, his position is without foundation. W. Holladay (*The Architecture of Jeremiah 1–20* [London: Associated University Press, 1976] 79-80 and *Jeremiah 1–25*, 310-11) offers a quite insightful analysis with attention to grammatical indicators and rhetorical structure. One problem with this passage involves whether the instruction to hear includes the instruction to teach or whether the instruction to teach is itself a citation of divine words, as the translation above indicates (cf. Jer 4:5 and n. 2 above). In either case, the final two bi-cola offer the content of the proposed lament.

en—perhaps the professionals summoned earlier—to teach their daughters and friends the art. The implication may be that the distress is of such magnitude that the professionals require auxiliary support. At any rate, another *qinah* fragment conveys the content of the proposed lament (v 20[21]). When YHWH speaks for yet a third time, he voices his own *qinah* mourning the slaughter of his people, instead of encouraging others to lament.

Finally, Jerusalem's spontaneous, anguished response to YHWH's announcement of impending disaster in Jer 4:19-21 finds close parallels in 10:19-21 and 13:22a. In these texts, Jerusalem reacts—without reflection or analysis—to the pain of her situation.

The Communal Confession of Sin

A second category of lament/confessional materials is the communal confession of sin: "We have sinned against YHWH/you." It occurs with much less frequency (in fact, not at all in Jer 4–6; see 3:22-25; 8:14-15; 14:7-9; 14:19-22). These confessions employ the same first-person plural forms of address which enticed interpreters of previous texts to develop intricate theories concerning the nature and degree of Jeremiah's empathy. However, commentators do not regard these confessions as evidence of a prophetic sense of empathetic guilt.

Two features of these confessions merit comment. First, like the cries of despair voiced by the community and Lady Zion, these confessions regularly appear in fast-paced dialogue. In Jer 3:21-25, for example, a narrator announces the sound of a voice crying out from the hills (v 21). YHWH offers the possibility of repentance and healing (v 22). The people confess their sin and announce their intention to return to their God (vv 23-25). No overt dialogue-markers such as the formulae "oracle of YHWH" or "thus says YHWH" assist the identification of speakers. Such rapid-fire alternation characterizes the poetry of the book of Jeremiah.[16]

Second, although they employ all the proper repentance language, the confessions of communal guilt also express a sense of confusion, resignation, and despair. From the standpoint of formally correct repentance,

---

[16]See J. Willis, "Dialogue Between Prophet and Audience as a Rhetorical Device in the Book of Jeremiah," *JSOT* 33 (1985): 63-82; cf. M. Biddle, *Redaction*, 72-76.

these are model confessions. They acknowledge guilt and embrace responsibility:

> Surely the hills are for naught,
>   the clamor on the mountains;
> Surely in YHWH our God
>   is the salvation of Israel.
> And Boshet has consumed
>   the produce of our fathers from our youth,
>   their flocks and their cattle,
>   their sons and their daughters.
> Let us lie down in our shame:
>   Our reproach covers us,
>   for against YHWH our God have we sinned,
>   we and our fathers from our youth to this day,
>   and we have not heeded the voice of YHWH our God.   (Jer 3:23-25)

From the perspective of a theological understanding of Judah's history, however, they seem to reflect a confusion resulting from the apparent conflict between YHWH's historic willingness to forgive and deliver and his apparent inability or unwillingness to do so in the current situation.

> Although our iniquities testify against us, YHWH,
>   act for your name's sake!
> Indeed, our apostasies are many,
>   against you have we sinned.
> O hope of Israel,
>   Savior in times of trouble,
> why should you be like a stranger in the land
>   and like a traveller bedding down for the night?
> Why should you be like an astonished man
>   like a champion unable to save?
> Rather, you are in our midst, YHWH
>   and we are called by your name, do not forsake us.   (Jer 14:7-9)

Indeed, this confusion concerning YHWH's fidelity to established patterns of behavior and to his promises results in despair. The people make no effort to rationalize or theologize; they simply resign themselves to their fate.

> Why are we sitting? Gather together!
>   Let's go to the fortified cities

and die there. YHWH our God has cut us off
   and given us poisonous water, for we sinned against YHWH.
We hope for peace to no avail,
   for a time of healing, and, behold, terror!   (Jer 8:14-15)

Divine Monologues

Divine monologues constitute a third significant category of lament in Jeremiah 7-20 (8:18-9:2[3]; 9:9-10[10-11]; 9:21[22]; 12:7-13; 13:15-17; 14:17-18; and 15:5-9). As with lament materials in Jeremiah 4–6, scholars tend to attribute these texts imprecisely to Jeremiah himself. M. Smith's assessment is typical:

> The tone of sympathy in chapters 7–10 belongs less to Yahweh than to the prophet; chapters 11–20 mark the loss of the prophet's sympathetic identification with the people. In these chapters the prophet's posture parallels the divine disposition [of wrath].[17]

Again as with lament materials in Jeremiah 4–6, however, the identification of Jeremiah as the speaker rests largely upon a priori assumptions. Rather, MT often explicitly designates Yahweh as speaker. In the end, the accumulation of examples renders the classic assessment untenable.

Jeremiah 8:18–9:2(3). Commentators usually describe the first and most difficult of these passages, 8:18–9:2(3), as a moving expression of Jeremiah's pain over the fate of his people.[18] Much recent research, however, noting a dialogue involving several interlocutors, modifies the standard approach. According to W. Holladay,[19] for example, the prophet speaks in Jer 8:18-21, quoting the people's complaint in v 19, and Yah-

---

[17]*Laments*, 65.

[18]J. Thompson's comment is typical: "Jeremiah was never a dispassionate observer of his nation's suffering, but entered into the anguish of the people and suffered with them. It is an open question whether the prophet is here projecting himself into the midst of a disaster about to overtake the people, or whether these words were uttered by the prophet at the time the disaster struck" (*Jeremiah*, 304); cf. W. Rudolph, *Jeremia*, 55.

[19]*Architecture*, 113.

weh speaks the remainder of the extended passage, 8:22–9:8(9).[20] R. Carroll assigns most of the unit to personified Jerusalem.[21]

Indeed, MT offers little reason to assign any portion of the passage to the prophet. First, although the abundant first person pronouns in this passage seem *prima faciae* ambiguous, MT explicitly identifies God and only God as speaker: "Why have they provoked me to anger?" (19b). Second, the oracular formula נְאֻם־יְהוָה in 8:17 and 9:2(3) demarcates 8:18–9:2(3) as an extended unit and suggests that, at least for MT, YHWH speaks the entire unit.[22] He cites the people in vv 19b and 20. Third, Jer

---

[20]J. Lundbom's analysis differs significantly from W. Holladay's only with reference to the latter half of the unit beginning in 8:22. He assigns parts of it to Jeremiah on the basis of the chiastic structure with reference to speakers in 8:18-21. According to Lundbom, Jeremiah speaks in v 18, the people in v 19a, YHWH in v 19b, the people again in v 20, and, finally, Jeremiah once again in v 21 (*Jeremiah: A Study in Ancient Hebrew Rhetoric*, SBLDS 18 [Missoula MT: Scholars Press, 1975] 84, 99). T. Polk (*Persona*, 109) is much more reticent. In his view, the unit begins with Jeremiah speaking and ends with Yahweh speaking, but the transition is difficult to pinpoint.

[21]*Jeremiah*, 233-34.

[22]R. Carroll's observations (*Jeremiah*, 235-36) on the question of the identity of the speaker here fail to recognize the dialogical nature of this passage. They are, however, very insightful concerning the problematic of literary personification:

[W]ho is the speaker? The lament for the city has already been encountered in 4.19-22 and there it was suggested that city or community might be the speaker. As this poem is very similar to that one, again the most likely speaker is the city (or the community speaking as the city). However, the city as speaker is but a metaphor; in reality somebody has to do the speaking. That somebody might be a priest, a prophet or a poet, and therefore a number of commentators treat the speaker as the prophet Jeremiah. Jeremiah speaks for or *as* the city. This is quite possible, but the logic of such an explanation requires it to be the city which is doing the speaking (Jeremiah is but the mouthpiece). It is therefore the city's pain which is spoken of rather than the individual speaker's pain. The people who are wounded (i.e. the community) are the wound of the city (cf. 30.12,15; 31.15). The personification of the city . . . in such poems does not mean that the speaker speaks of his own feelings; he speaks of the city's responses to the disaster. . . . It is an illegitimate move to argue from these poems to the

8:23(9:1) closely parallels YHWH's statement in 14:17-18 ("eyes run with tears day and night," "virgin daughter of my people," "wound"; cf. "no knowledge" motif in 9:2[3] and 14:18). Fourth, the phrase "my people" appears outside 8:18–9:2(3) in YHWH's denunciation of the religious leadership (Jer 8:11) and in the divine lament in Jer 15:5-9 (v 7). Fifth, the parallel structure of the rhetorical questions in vv 19b,c and 22 (מַדּוּעַ ... אִם ... הַ) suggests that both sets involve the same pair of speakers: "Is the Lord not in Zion?" || "Is there no balm in Gilead"—both spoken by the people; and "Why have they provoked me?" || "Why have they not been healed?"—both spoken by YHWH. Finally, Jer 8:18–9:2(3) resembles the dialogue in Jeremiah 4 exhibiting (a) shifts in speaker sometimes without explicit markers, but always implied by context, and (b) only two participants. The dialogical structure of Jer 8:18–9:2(3) may be represented, then, as follows:

YHWH
> My joy is gone, grief is upon me, my heart is sick.
>> Hark, the cry of my poor people from far and wide in the land:

People
> "Is the Lord not in Zion? Is her king not in her?"

YHWH
> Why [then] have they provoked me to anger with their images,
>> with their foreign idols?

People
> "The harvest is past, the summer is ended,
>> and we are not saved."

YHWH
> For the hurt of my poor people I am hurt,
>> I mourn, and dismay has taken hold of me.

People
> "Is there no balm in Gilead? Is there no physician there?"

YHWH
> Why then has the health of my poor people not been restored?
>> O that my head were a spring of water.   (NRSV)

The tension inherent in this quite dramatic interplay of voices highlights the irreconcilable frames of reference of the participants. YHWH

---

personal feelings of Jeremiah or to cite them as evidence for the oneness of feeling and identity between Jeremiah and his people.

speaks to the people's determination to sin and their inability to perceive their sin as an obstacle to relationship with YHWH. The people, on the other hand, focus on their disappointment in *YHWH's* unresponsiveness.

Jeremiah 9:9-10(10-11). The standard approach to Jer 9:9-10(10-11) accepts the LXX, Syr and Lat plural imperative reading "Take up" in v 9 and understands the verb as God's instruction to the people. J. Thompson[23] and W. McKane[24] retain MT but consider LXX, Syr, and Lat the result of the mistaken assumption that YHWH speaks. If Jeremiah speaks, the problem posed by YHWH's pain dissolves. By considering vv 9 (10) and 10 (11) separate fragments, a lament and an announcement of destruction, J. Bright[25] and R. Carroll[26] avoid the problem.

A growing number of exegetes support a third option. The context implies that YHWH himself voices the lament in Jer 9:9-10(10-11). P. Kelly[27] comments that the anthropomorphic image of YHWH "weeping and wailing" may be too distasteful for some. Yet, MT's straightforward intention is difficult to gainsay. Throughout Jeremiah 9, MT indicates YHWH as speaker. The oracular formulae in vv 2, 6, 8, 12, 14, 16, 19, 21, 22, 23, 24 (English 3, 7, 9, 13, 15, 17, 20, 22, 23, 24, 26), God's repeated charge that the people have failed or refused to "know me" (vv 2, 6 [English 3, 7]), and the formula "therefore thus says the Lord" (v 6 [English 7]) leave no doubt concerning the speaker's identity, at least not from MT's perspective. Furthermore, the *qinah* meter in v 9c(10c) continues in v 10a(11a) and v 10a relates syntactically to the preceding by means of the initial waw-consecutive,[28] suggesting that vv 9-10(10-11) should be read as a single divine lament. Finally, this divine lament expresses a sentiment comparable to that expressed in Jer 12:7-13 and 15:5-9, texts generally acknowledged as divine speech.[29]

---

[23]*Jeremiah*, 312n.6: *"Since Jeremiah is the speaker, MT seems preferable"* [emphasis added].

[24]*Jeremiah*, 203-204; cf. J. Lundbom, *Rhetoric*, 84, 99.

[25]*Jeremiah: Introduction, Translation, and Notes*, AB 21 (Garden City NY: Doubleday, 1965) 72-73.

[26]*Jeremiah*, 241-42.

[27]P. Craigie, et al., *Jeremiah*, 143.

[28]P. Craigie, et al., *Jeremiah*, 118.

[29]M. Smith ("Jeremiah IX 9—A Divine Lament," *VT* 37 [1987]: 97-99) suggests an additional argument based on CTA 5 (KTU 1.5).VI.25—CTA 6

For the mountains, take up weeping and wailing
    and for the open pastures a qinah,
because they are devastated so that no one passes through
    and the sound of cattle is not heard;
Birds of the air, indeed all animals
    have fled and gone.

I will make Jerusalem a ruin,
    a jackal den,
and the cities of Judah I will desolate
    without inhabitant.   (Jer 9:9-10[10-11])

Jeremiah 9:21(22). The divine lament in Jer 9:21(22) received preliminary treatment above.[30] Two additional observations are pertinent at
this point, however. First, the entirety of Jer 9:16-21(17-22) manifests an
involved discourse matrix. Frequent divine-speech markers indicate that,
from the perspective of the final form/redaction of the text, the entire unit
purports to be YHWH-speech. *Within* these divine sayings, YHWH proposes
statements for other figures. A redaction-critical perspective might
suggest that a series of originally independent (cultic?) units have been
combined through the inclusion of the divine-speech markers. Strikingly,
the final form of the text, however, results in a characterization of YHWH
which emphasizes the divine pathos. The concluding divine lament only
makes explicit this divine pain. In it, YHWH does not propose lament
speech for others: YHWH laments.

Jeremiah 12:7-13. Since scholarship generally regards Jer 12:7-13 as
a divine lament,[31] it requires only brief treatment here.

(KTU 1.6).I.7 which records Anat's lament "over" her lover.

[30]Pp. 24-27.

[31]J. Thompson (*Jeremiah*, 356) comments: "Yahweh laments his ravaged
inheritance"; cf. D. Bak, *Klagender*, 33-36. M. Smith (*Laments*, 48), following
A. Diamond (*Confessions*, 153, 156), argues that "the divine pain expressed in
12:7-13 parallels the prophetic experience conveyed in the preceding prophetic
lament . . . "; so also P. Craigie, et al., *Jeremiah*, 184. W. Rudolph (*Jeremia*, 75)
and W. McKane (*Jeremiah*, 268) suggest that the placement of these verses may
have resulted from an improper understanding of Jeremiah as speaker.

I forsake my house;
    I leave my heritage;
I give the darling of my life
    into the hands of her enemies.

My heritage is to me
    like a lion in the forest.
She cries out against me,
    therefore I despise her.

Is my heritage a bird of prey to me?
    Are birds of prey surrounding her?[32]
Go, gather all the beasts of the field!
    Bring them to devour her!

Many shepherds destroy my vineyard;
    They trample my portion.
They make my lovely portion
    a desolate wilderness.

They make it desolate;
    Desolate it mourns to me.
The whole land is desolate
    for no one takes it to heart.

On all the bare heights in the wilderness
    destroyers come.
For YHWH's sword devours
    from one end of the land to the other:
No peace for all flesh.

They sow wheat and reap thorns;
    They wear themselves out to no profit.

---

[32]The text here is very difficult. At issue are the meanings of עַיִט ("bird of prey" or "rabid") and צָבוּעַ ("speckled" or "hyena"). Proposals for translating the passage abound. The translation offered above is an attempt to respect the extant text of MT. For a thorough discussion of proposed translations and emendations, see W. McKane, 269-73.

> They are disappointed by their harvests
> > because of YHWH's burning anger.   (Jer 12:7-13)

As in previous passages, YHWH refers repeatedly to his people in tender terms, "my house," "my heritage," "the beloved of my heart" (12:7-10; cf. 8:18, 19, 21, 22, 23[9:1]; 9:1[2]). He describes the effects of Judah's sin on the environment in terms of desolation, destruction, and abandonment (12:7, 9-12; cf. 9:9-10[10-11]). He explains that the harvest in which the people had placed such hope (8:20) has proven disastrous (12:13). Sadly, they have brought all this upon themselves (12:13; cf. 8:19; 9:1-2[2-3]).

Jeremiah 13:15-17. Readings of Jer 13:15-17 reflect the established pattern. Despite the explicit declaration that YHWH speaks vv 15-17 with no subsequent signals to the contrary, scholars usually regard v 17 as an interjection of prophetic emotion. For example, while McKane admits that there may be "an element of 'word of Yahweh' in vv. 15-17," he contends that v 17 would then be

> a personal postscript by Jeremiah, touched with anguish, in which he makes his last appeal: if you refuse to listen to Yahweh's word, sorrow will cut me to the quick.[33]

Admittedly, the weeping prophet figure would find strong support here but for the text's specific claim to be YHWH speech.

> Hear and give ear!
> > Do not be arrogant: YHWH speaks.
> "Give glory to YHWH your God
> > before it grows dark;
> And before your feet stumble
> > on the mounts at twilight;
> And you hope for light
> > and it turns to gloom
> > > and becomes deep darkness.

---

[33]*Jeremiah*, 302; cf. W. Rudolph (*Jeremia*, 82-83) who argues that YHWH speaks this word his prophet, but that when it comes to pass "dann wird der Prophet nicht triumphieren, sondern bittere Tränen vergiessen"; cf. also J. Thompson, *Jeremiah*, 369. In R. Carroll's view (*Jeremiah*, 300) the MT of v 17 refers to the individual while LXX refers to community.

> But if you will not listen
> [In secret][34]
> My soul will weep because of your pride;
> It will cry bitterly.
> And my eyes will shed tears
> because YHWH's flock has been captured."   (Jer 13:15-17)

YHWH certainly expresses similar sentiment elsewhere (cf. YHWH's "weeping eyes" in 8:23). Furthermore, God's third person self-references in vv 16-18 ("Give glory to YHWH your God," for example) reflect a common Biblical solution to the rhetorical problem of reporting the words of God (compare Exod 20:7, 10; 24:1,2; Num 19:1; Deut 1:36; Josh 1:9; 1 Sam 10:19; 2 Sam 12:9; Isa 1:4; 3:16-17; 28:21-22; 31:4-5; Jer 23:16-17; 31:2-3, 11-12 for just a few of the many texts in which YHWH refers to himself in the third person). In fact, difficulties with the text and translation of verbs in v 16 may suggest a history of scribal uncertainty as to whether and how to preserve the unit as YHWH speech.[35] Only circular reasoning, however, can contend that Jeremiah should or must be understood as the speaker of v 17: texts such as Jer 13:17 indicate that Jeremiah suffered emotionally from the message he was called to preach; since Jeremiah suffered so, texts such as Jer 13:17 can be understood as Jeremiah speech, although they offer no explicit indication to that effect. Given the direct attribution of vv 16-17 to God and the Hebrew Bible's practice of divine self-reference in the third person, the burden of proof rests upon interpretations which seek to contradict contention of the text that the reader should "hear and give ear . . . YHWH speaks" (13:15).

---

[34]It is very difficult to determine whether בְּמִסְתָּרִים should be read with the first or the second clause. MT's punctuation includes it in the second phrase, although metrical considerations would suggest inclusion in the first. The versions and commentators are divided. For a useful survey of the alternatives, see W. McKane, *Jeremiah*, 299.

[35]The hiphil יֶחְשֹׁף is an internal causative (cf. GKC 73f). וְשָׂמָה and יְשִׂית present a range of difficulties. Only here and in Job 36:32 is אוֹר construed as a feminine. The conjunction is awkward. *Qere* reads the final verb as a passive participle, which conforms to the understanding of the passage as YHWH-speech, instead of as *Kethib's* strange mixed form.

Jeremiah 14:17-18. Scholars have difficulty establishing the genre of Jer 14:17-18. For example, W. Rudolph[36] considers it a prophetic lament, J. Thompson[37] "a description of the plague," and M. Smith[38] and K. O'Connor[39] describe it as "judgment" language, although O'Connor later refers to it as "a poetic lament of the prophet (or Yahweh)."[40]

And say to them this Word:

> "Let my eyes pour tears
>   night and day without ceasing:
> The virgin, the daughter of my people, is shattered
>   with a great jolt,
>   a very severe blow.
> If I go into the field—
>   Look! Those slain by the sword—
> If I enter the city—
>   Look! Diseases of famine—
> For both prophet and priest
>   travel around the land, but they know nothing."   (Jer 14:17-18)

The problem revolves around two issues. First, although the introduction, "You shall say to them this word," indicates that YHWH speech follows, scholars consider the ideas expressed in vv 17b-18 more appropriate to the prophet than to God. J. Bright, for example, deems the introduction "an editorial transition in the style of the prose passage preceding, linking it to the poem that follows—which is not an oracle."[41] Similarly, W. McKane considers the introduction "as inappropriate as the one which introduces vv. 2-9."[42] The redactor who contributed the introduction may well have been responsible for the placement of the entire unit, however. Thus, T. Polk[43] and others[44] accept the introduction as an integral con-

---

[36]*Jeremia*, 87.

[37]*Jeremiah*, 385.

[38]*Laments*, 51.

[39]*Confessions*, 106n.22.

[40]*Confessions*, 136.

[41]*Jeremiah*, 101.

[42]*Jeremiah*, 329. Cf. also D. Bak, *Klagender*, 56, who seems satisfied to dismiss the introduction as a "redactional addition."

[43]*Persona*, 96-97.

stiituent of the final form of the text, but rely upon a nuanced understanding of the prophet's identification with YHWH to explain this unit and others like it as *both* prophetic *and* divine speech: YHWH speaks through the prophet, the prophet mirrors the heart of God. This approach, while faithful to the text of the introduction, misconstrues the text of the body of the unit. How does the text indicate, explicitly or implicitly, that Jeremiah speaks?

Interpreters often appeal to form-critical criteria in support of the contention that this lament (originally) voiced Jeremiah's pain. W. McKane comments:

> Verses 17-18 will not pass for a constituent part of a communal lament. They may have been pressed into service in order to provide a description of distress which triggers the appeal to Yahweh in vv. 19ff., but this is not their original function. . . . They deal with private sorrow . . . but they do not lead on naturally to a prayer in which 1st person plural suffixes and verbs appear.[45]

Such appeals raise a second difficulty, however, namely the context of this language in a prophetic career. The rhetorical function of this language does not fit neatly into the categories of prophetic speech. K. Pohlmann[46] observes, correctly, that

> the fact that the texts in question are addressed both directly and exclusively to Yahweh, although now as components of a prophetic book are addressed to the public while the form of prayers addressed to Yahweh is maintained, requires explanation to the extent that one must assume that Jeremiah, himself, provided his Yahweh-oriented laments, whose proper place and function were in private dialogue with Yahweh, with an additional function in or for the public; otherwise these texts would have been unavailable to a third party and thus untransmittable. What function, however, could that have been?

Theoretically, Jer 14:17b-18 could be understood against its original or its literary setting. Form-critical criteria, applied consistently, suggest

---

[44]M. Woudstra, "A Prophet to the Nations: Reflections on Jeremiah's Call to the Prophetic Office," *VR* 18 (1972): 2; D. Bak, *Klagender*, 181-84.

[45]*Jeremiah*, 331.

[46]*Ferne Gottes*, 4.

no satisfactory original public setting for this private language. Nor do literary criteria direct attention to the prophet's private life. Instead, the literary setting depicts Jer 14:17-18 as YHWH-speech. Furthermore, in response to McKane's objection concerning the awkward placement of Jer 14:17-18, it can be observed that this lament, understood as YHWH-speech, elicits a communal response: "Have *you* totally rejected Judah?" (14:19). YHWH's admission of his sorrow at the fate of his people provokes an appeal for mercy or an expression of despair at the finality of YHWH's decision.

Jeremiah 15:5-9. Jer 15:5-9, widely recognized as a divine lament, presents an instructive case study in the force of status quo interpretations.

> Who will spare you, Jerusalem?
>   And who will mourn you?
> Who will turn aside to ask
>   of your welfare?

> You forsook me—saying of YHWH—
>   You walked backwards.
> I reach out my hand against you and ruin you
>   I am weary of compassion.

> I will winnow them with a pitch fork
>   in the gates of the land.
> I will make childless; I will destroy my people.
>   They do not turn from their ways.

> Their widows are more numerous to me
>   than the sand of the sea.
> I will bring against them—the mother of young mem—
>   destroyers at noonday.

> I will cause suddenly to fall against her
>   —the city—sudden terror.
> She who bore seven will faint,
>   gasping for breath.

> Her sun sets while it is yet day.
>   She is ashamed and abashed.

And I give their remant to the sword
before their enemies   —saying of YHWH.

Several features already noted in disputed divine laments such as Jer
8:18–9:1(2) recur here: the unit begins as a first person $qinah$;[47] two oracular formulae explicitly indicate the unit as YHWH-speech (vv 6,9); it ad-
mixes address (vv 5-6) and soliloquy (vv 7-9); characteristically, YHWH
speaks to and about Jerusalem and the people; he describes Jerusalem as
a bereaved widow and mother and refers to the people as עַמִּי (cf.
8:11,19, 21,22,23[9:1];9:1[9:2]; 14:17); and נֶפֶשׁ functions as the feminine subject of a verbal clause. W. McKane, who acknowledges several
of these features, attributes the entire unit to YHWH.[48] P. Kelly calls attention to parallels between 15:5-9 and 9:1-10[2-11].[49] Why do scholars persist in attributing to Jeremiah other passages very similar to Jer 15:5-9?

Summary Conclusions regarding YHWH-laments. This analysis of the
six YHWH-laments in Jeremiah 6–20 suggests two summary observations.
First, several texts do not readily submit to form-critical analysis: most,
if not all, would be anonymous and acontextual apart from literary
settings identifying the speaking "I" as YHWH (cf. 9:9-10[10-11]; 13:15-
17; 14:17-18). Assuming the accuracy of contemporary understandings
of the formation of prophetic books, these texts *may* stem from some
public setting. Nevertheless, given the current state of the book, it is
dangerous to draw conclusions about the psychospiritual state of the historical prophet on the basis of snippets of emotionally laden language
which come to us with no clue as to their original contexts. More probably, given the difficulty in imagining *Sitz im Leben* for these texts, they
can only be explained in terms of literary activity. In this case, however,
it is inconsistent to persist in describing Jeremiah as a literary character
in precisely the same terms older scholarship used in biographies of the

---

[47]Cf. J. Berridge, *Prophet, People, and Word of Yahweh: An Examination of
Form and Content in the Proclamation of the Prophet Jeremiah*, BST 4 (Zürich:
EVZ-Verlag, 1970) 176-79.

[48]*Jeremiah*, 337.

[49]P. Craigie, et al., *Jeremiah*, 200.

prophet.[50] On a literary level, all of these speeches are assigned specifically and explicitly to YHWH.

Second, the literary function of these YHWH-speeches can perhaps best be described in terms of characterization and dialogue. Although the modern reader of Jeremiah 4 or 14 knows, on one level, that an author/redactor produced the speeches in these dialogues, the integrity of the dialogue partners as literary characters must be respected. How can the interpreter ascertain which, if any, of the speakers represent the viewpoint of the author/redactor/prophet, real or implied? Who speaks with Twain's voice or the narrator's, Huck or Jim?[51] The composite personae which result from disregarding explicit dialogue markers in the text are at best artificial constructs owing more to the interpreter's presupposition than to attention to literary technique.

Characterization of the Participants in the Dialogue

The speakers identified in the analysis above represent markedly discrete perspectives on the problem addressed in the book of Jeremiah. The opening chapters of the book raise the question of the possibilities for and parameters of continued relationship between God and God's wayward people. Several principles, each apparently reasonable and internally consistent but difficult to reconcile with one another, struggle to reach equilibrium. God's chosen people sin, pushing God's patience beyond its limits. Yet God, remembering his promise and love, finds it painful to punish. Faced with the specter of God's wrath, the people react in dismay, pain, and simple confession. Ultimately, the canonical book of Jeremiah fails to resolve these tensions. In fact, the case could be made that the *argument* of the book lies in the contention that God's relationship with God's people defies resolution and systematization.

---

[50]T. Polk *(Persona,* 80) suggests almost the contrary position with reference to the nature of prophetic intercession. He argues, "One stands for others precisely as *oneself.* One's own self in its full range of aspects and qualities must remain in place in order to stand in for others. . . . It follows that one must own the 'I' one speaks in order for it even to begin to representative"; cf. n. 22, above.

[51]Cf. M. Smith, *Laments,* 50-51; A. Diamond, *Confessions,* 63, 158, 161; and R. Carroll, *Jeremiah,* 235.

The People

The voice of the people, heard primarily in expressions of fearful dismay and nonspecific confessions of guilt, seems to represent a position which has not grasped the full implications of the situation. With few exceptions, the people's statements can all be summarized with the rather stereotypical expressions "Woe to us! We are destroyed!" and "We have sinned!"[52]

In a departure from the norm, Jer 8:14-15 apparently acknowledges the futility of repentance and confession since God has already reached an irrevocable decision. Two confessions in Jeremiah 14 (vv 7-9, 19-22) go several steps further. Although they, too, offer no solutions to the Jeremianic dilemma of sin and forgiveness, they succeed at least in stating the problem clearly and pointedly. On the one hand, both texts acknowledge the long history of Judah's sin (14:7,20). On the other hand, both propose rather forceful theological arguments as claims on God's mercy (14:7b, 10, 21-22). The people appeal to God "to act for [his] name's sake" (14:7, 9, 21) and to remember the covenant (14:21). They offer doxologies to YHWH as savior in troubled times (14:8), Israel's hope (14:8, 22) and the only God able to send rain (14:22). But the conventional appeals prove ineffective, so the people also express the profound confusion characteristic of Hebrew complaints: "Why should you be like . . . a mighty warrior who cannot help?" (14:9); "Why have you struck us down so that there is no healing for us?" (14:19). The people, then, voice only the pain of catastrophe, dismay at its ferocity, guilt for the role their sins played in provoking God's anger, and confusion over God's apparent unwillingness to relent.

The communal confessions present interpreters of the book of Jeremiah with a peculiar problem. If one seeks a historical setting in the life of Jeremiah against which to set these confessions, one is forced to regard them as insincere, cynical, or inadequate in some way. No overt marks of insincerity, cynicism, or inadequacy are apparent in these confessions, however. Only the interpreter's awareness that YHWH apparently did not forgive Judah's sin, that the Babylonians devastated Judah and Jerusalem, suggests such an interpretation. If, on the other hand, they are

---

[52]Cf. M. Biddle, *Redaction*, 75.

seen as fragments of laments from shortly after or during the crisis, for example, anachronistically included alongside earlier materials, the key to interpreting them must be sought in something other than the historical course of events. Significantly, the final redaction of the book of Jeremiah is also aware of the historical outcome of the Babylonian crisis. Indeed, the final redaction of the book includes passages such as Jer 15:1-4, which seems to represent a retrospective viewpoint of the Babylonian crisis as the expression of a divine decision predating Jeremiah's ministry. In effect, the final form of the book excludes any possibility of repentance for preexilic Judah.[53] Furthermore, the final form of the book casts many of these statements ultimately as proposed statements within divine sayings.

If the book of Jeremiah understands that no repentance was possible, how do these communal confessions function? Apparently, the final form of the book intends to model the proper response to YHWH's judgment. Passages such as Jer 3:22-25 offer *canonical* paradigms for God's people.[54]

City

Similar observations may be made regarding the characterization of Lady Jerusalem in Jeremiah. Her voice lacks even the slight theological nuance heard on occasion from the people. She speaks only to cry out in terror and pain: "I'm fainting before killers!" (4:31); "Oh the walls of my heart!" (4:19); "my curtains . . . " (4:20). She makes no effort to defend herself against the charges brought against her; she does not attempt an analysis of the situation which prevails in her relationship with YHWH; she merely reacts to her plight.

God

God, by far the most interesting character in these dialogues, voices pathos and conflict, an internal struggle between anger and sympathy. In dialogue with personified Jerusalem, YHWH adopts an angry, almost

---

[53]J. McConville (*Judgment and Promise: An Interpretation of the Book of Jeremiah* [Winona Lake: Eisenbrauns, 1993] 40) comments in reference to Jeremiah 3 that, "In any case, the reflection on the theme of repentance knows of Judah's ultimate and decisive failure to repent."

[54]M. Biddle, *Redaction*, 83-121.

vengeful tone. Consistent with the tone of an extensive body of materials addressed to Lady Jerusalem in Jeremiah 2,[55] YHWH repeatedly and forcefully accuses the city of the vilest infidelity and immorality:

Oh Jerusalem! Wash you heart clean of wickedness. . . .   (Jer 4:14)

Your ways and your doings have brought this upon you!   (Jer 4:18)

And you, Destroyed, what are you doing?
    . . . futilely you beautify yourself:
    your lovers seek your life.   (Jer 4:30-31)

I myself will lift up your skirts over your head
    and your shame will be seen!   (Jer 13:26)

YHWH seems bent on humiliating Jerusalem for her infidelity and appears determined to press the point that Jerusalem has brought all this on herself. She is guilty: God acts justly.

In sharp contrast, YHWH also expresses sorrow over the suffering inflicted on the people. Indeed, YHWH suffers grief and dismay. The people's plaintive cries of distress in Jer 8:18-9:2(3), which question YHWH's continued presence with Zion and the ability or willingness of YHWH to save, elicit responses from YHWH which manifest his emotional and relational predicament. In a rhetorical response to the people's question about his devotion to Zion, YHWH asks why the people have forced him to punish. When the people resignedly declare that their hopes for salvation have gone unfulfilled, YHWH reasserts his own sensitivity to their pain. In answer to the people's almost bitter question concerning the disappointed expectation of healing, YHWH takes up the idea of health and redefines it in terms of fundamental well-being: "I share your interest in health; while you mean the removal of this pain, I long for the restoration of our relationship and your return to obedience." In the end, frustrated that the people recognize only the symptom of illness and not its root cause—and therefore unable to spare them from judgment—YHWH wishes only to weep.

Themes sounded in Jer 8:18–9:2(3) recur in the other divine laments: God returns frequently to the image of the people's "wound" and the

---

[55]See M. Biddle, *Redaction*, 39-82 and the discussion below, 66-72.

parallel "wound" in his own heart (8:21-22; 14:17; cf. 8:11). He refers repeatedly and delicately to "my house" (12:7), "my people" (8:19,21,22), "my heritage" (12:7,8), "my vineyard" (12:10), and so on. He agonizes again and again over the people's obstinate rebellion which provoked his anger. Why have they persisted in their sin (8:19; 15:6-7; compare 8:5)? Finally, God weeps for his people (8:23[9:1]; 13:17) and with them (9:18)—*Pater Doloroso*!

Prophet

The remarkable near-silence of the prophet qua individual must merely be noted at this point. Subsequent chapters will focus attention on the prophet's so-called "confessions" and on the prose materials which deal with the prophet's intercessory role. These chapters will examine the significance of the explicitly prophetic voice in relation to other voices in Jeremiah.

Contours of the Dialogue

Confessional materials in Jeremiah 7–10 fall into three major categories: responses to crisis, communal confessions, and first-person laments, which may be subdivided into divine laments, laments of other leading figures (Lady Zion, for example), and prophetic confessions. Explicit textual indicators require the modification of common interpretations of two of these categories. Varieties of the relatively frequent "Woe is us/me" cry appear in dialogues, reported or envisioned, involving YHWH and the people or the city. Nothing points to Jeremiah as the speaker of these cries. Similarly, the texts of the first person laments imply, both explicitly and contextually, that YHWH speaks. Form-critical considerations undergird the conclusion that YHWH speaks directly in these texts: it is difficult to identify *Sitz im Leben des Volkes* for these very private utterances. Positing *Sitz im Leben Jeremias*, it is then difficult to account for the public transmission of these private utterances. Alternatively, *Sitz im Buch* provided by the editors and redactors of the Jeremiah tradition are readily apparent. YHWH speaks these laments in dialogue with the people. The assumption that these laments provide either a glimpse into the prophet's private life or the components for a literary persona raises the question of prophetic disobedience. Finally, these divine laments characterize Jeremiah 7–15; the so-called prophetic confessions dominate only in Jeremiah 15–20. Clearly, scholarly preoccupation with the confessions misdirects. Jeremiah 7–10 should be analyzed as part of Jeremiah 7–20, and the "miscellaneous" lament materials distributed throughout these chapters should be recognized as vital components in a complex structural polyphony.

To return to a question raised earlier concerning the structural role of Jeremiah 7–10, the accompanying table (see page 46) illustrates that, in addition to the superscription, prose sermon/narrative, etc., pattern detailed above, lament materials in Jeremiah 7–10 bear greater resemblance to similar materials in Jer 11–16:9, in particular, than in Jeremiah 4–6. W. Holladay's designation, "Supplementary Foe Cycle," acknowledges similarities between Jeremiah 4–6 and 8–10. Nevertheless, the term fails to account for the fact that two other categories of lament materials in Jeremiah 7–10 occur in 7–15 only. The distribution of communal confessions of sin (8:14-15; 14:7-9, 19-22) and divine laments (8:18–9:2; 9:9-10; 12:7-13; 13:15-17; 14:17-18; 15:5-9) suggests no major break between Jeremiah 10 and 11, Holladay's "Curse Framework" notwithstanding.[56]

Furthermore, the usual characterization of the "confessions of Jeremiah" as the governing element of Jeremiah 11–20 seems, in the end, inappropriate. The confessions dominate only chapters 17–20; the interchange between the frightened, pleading people and their heartbroken, resigned God dominates chapters 7–16.

---

[56]*Architecture*, 160-62; K. O'Connor, *Confessions*, 131; M. Smith, *Laments*, 2, among others. The curses announced in Jer 11:3 and Jer 20:5 are very dissimilar. In the former God addresses those who fail to keep the covenant; in the latter the prophet addresses the one who heralded his birth. The former finds a better thematic parallel in the curse in Jer 17:5 and the latter in the curse in Jer 15:10.

COMMUNAL LAMENTS	COMMUNAL CONFESSIONS	DIVINE LAMENTS	PROPHETIC "CONFESSIONS"	PROHIBITIONS
4:5-8				
4:13				
4:19-22				
4:31				
6:4				
6:24-25				
				7:16-20
7:29				
	8:14-15			
		8:18–9:2		
		9:9-10		
9:16-20				
10:19-21				
				11:14
			11:18-20; 12:1-4	
		12:7-13		
		13:15-17		
	14:7-9			
				14:11-12
		14:17-18		
	14:19-22			
		15:5-9		
			15:10-18	
				16:5-9
			17:14-18	
			18:18-23	
			20:7-12	
			20:14-17	

YHWH's Resolve and Prophetic Complaint: Discourse Concerning Justice

In comparison to the materials examined immediately above, there are striking contrasts in the tone and substance of texts in which YHWH addresses the prophet individually. If the interaction between the people and YHWH in Jeremiah 7–16 depicts a distressed, bewildered people and a disconsolate, resigned deity, the interchange between the prophet and YHWH reveals a resolutely angry deity in dialogue with a relatively quiet, yet petulant prophet whose primary contribution to the discussion explores the character and scope of divine justice.

Counter to a long tradition of Jeremianic scholarship, the present analysis of dialogue involving these two voices challenges the notion of an evolution of thought in the book from an optimism about the possibility for repentance to a resignation in the face of disaster. The traditional approach holds that a development in Jeremiah's message may be discerned in the structure of the book. T. Raitt suggests, for example, that strong words of judgment together with words of hope and calls to repentance characterized Jeremiah's early preaching. During a subsequent transitional phase, the people's failure to repent in response to Jeremiah's preaching became the grounds for impending judgment. Finally, after a caesura roughly coinciding with the Babylonian disaster, Jeremiah began to preach a message of unqualified salvation.[1]

C. Seitz also sees evidence of such a sequence in the structure of the book. In his view Jeremiah 1–6 reflect the period when Jeremiah still

---

[1]*A Theology of Exile: Judgment/Deliverance in Jeremiah and Ezekiel* (Philadelphia: Fortress, 1977) 36; J. Unterman (*From Repentance to Redemption: Jeremiah's Thought in Transition* [Sheffield: JSOT Press, 1987]) holds a very similar view.

considered repentance a possibility. Jeremiah 7–20, on the other hand, portray the shift in God's attitude from patience to anger. Even the prophet, sympathetic toward the people in Jeremiah 7–10, loses patience with them in chapters 11–20.[2]

From a meta-discursive perspective, however, dialogue between YHWH and the prophet concerning Judah's fate primarily offers the narrator-redactor's perspective into the mind of God. As the confessions, which constitute a component of it, this conversation, as whole, reports presumably private communications that often have no clear setting in the public ministry of the prophet. Thus, a second approach notes this basic paradox embodied in its final form and emphasizes the redactional process that resulted in the final shape of the book. According to E. Nicholson, for example, the final product owes much to Deuteronomistic redactors working in the Exile.[3]

J. McConville, while denying that the book reflects a chronological development in Jeremiah's preaching, discerned a theological structure that embodies Jeremiah's mature reflection on his ministry and on the books of Deuteronomy, Hosea, and some part of the Deuteronomistic History. Although Jeremiah may have, at some point early in his career, preached in expectation of Judah's repentance, the composite nature of the book makes it very difficult to ascertain a historical setting in the prophet's career against which to read specific passages. Instead, the compiler of the book—and McConville sees no reason to deny that role

---

[2]C. Seitz, "The Prophet Moses and the Canonical Shape of Jeremiah," *ZAW* 101 (1989): 8-9; cf. M. Smith, *Laments*, 65.

[3]*Preaching to the Exiles*; D. Jobling ("The Quest of the Historical Jeremiah," 287) succinctly summarizes Nicholson's position as follows:

The preaching ascribed to Jeremiah exhibits a paradox; doom is certain, but repentance is possible. In Jeremiah's own situation the contradiction would be irresoluble; but in Nicholson's view the true audience is the exilic one, and for them the two sides of the paradox are equally necessary. Before the Exile, the punishment was sealed. But the possibility of repentance *now*, after the blow has fallen, is the only basis of hope. Thus Jeremiah is *allowed* to say what he said to his own time, and is simultaneously *made* to say a new word for a new time.

to Jeremiah himself—has arranged the whole with a view to a retrospective theological assessment of events in Judah's Babylonian experience.[4]

From a source perspective, these exchanges between YHWH and the prophet largely coincide with the prose material identified by Nicholson and others as "deuteronomistic" and described as postcrisis theological reflection on the significance of the historical catastrophe.[5] Yet, differences between certain of YHWH's public suggestions and YHWH's private communications to the prophet, on the one hand, and issues related to YHWH's justice raised by the prophet in response, on the other, challenge presumptions that this prose material in the book of Jeremiah represents a unified perspective and that the *Gerichtsdoxologie* motif of Jeremianic prose focuses solely on justifying YHWH's course of action in the Babylonian crisis. YHWH speaks in at least three voices in the book: in poetry YHWH mourns Judah's fate, in prose YHWH privately denies hope or publicly offers it.

Basic Assumptions

In the end, the thoroughgoing redactional work which produced the book renders the question of the historical prophet's preaching of repentance virtually irresoluble. Similarly, the text's concentration on YHWH's static viewpoint stymies the question of a progression of thought on the literary level: YHWH's firm intention to punish Judah is established from the outset and rather consistently maintained throughout the book.[6] Several entangled issues require attention, and several assumptions of earlier research must be rejected.

Despite persistent attempts, the assumption that the book of Jeremiah preserves the prophet's preaching in some chronological order simply

---

[4]*Judgment and Promise*, 24-26, 36-41.

[5]The dialogue between YHWH and Jeremiah occurs primarily in the so-called "C" or "prose sermon" material. Although scholars disagree as to the origins of this material, it is usually described in terms of its clear affinity with deuteronomistic prose. Compare, e.g., W. Thiel, *Redaktion* and E. Nicholson, *Preaching to the Exiles*. Concerning the characteristic deuteronomistic interest in justifying YHWH's Babylonian judgment on Judah (*Gerichtsdoxologie*), see, e.g., O. Steck, *Israel und das gewaltsame Geschick der Propheten*.

[6]See Jer 1:13-19; 3:6-10; 5:7-9; 6:27-30; in addition to the texts treated below.

cannot be sustained, principally because no reliable criteria have been established for assigning materials that appear early in the book to the early period in Jeremiah's ministry. A recent example illustrates the problem. With regard to the question of the prophetic *ipsissima verba*, K. Seybold[7] employs crucial criteria only slightly modified from those of B. Duhm's turn-of-the-century commentary. Poetry can be assumed to be authentic, especially in view of the personal tone of the confessions and the presumptive reliability of Jeremiah's friend and scribe, Baruch. Employing a time-honored approach, Seybold groups texts by chronology and genre. Jeremiah's earliest activity during Josiah's reign focused on the former Northern kingdom and produced a series of short sayings and poems now collected in Jeremiah 2–3 and 30–31. Seybold discerns a development in Jeremiah's literary technique during this period from short sayings, to short poems, and finally to the extended poem found in Jeremiah 30–31. During the second period of Jeremiah's activity, his preaching in the context of the Babylonian threat, Jeremiah employed a range of literary genre: critical commentaries on Judah's institutions (temple, monarchy, prophecy, and wisdom), "visions" concerning the Northern enemy, the nations, and the death of Jerusalem, prophetic symbolic acts, and self-referential genre such as the confessions.

While Seybold's assumptions have honorable pedigrees, they are limited in their usefulness. First, the authenticity of poetry can only be assumed, not demonstrated, and this assumption does not recognize the possibility of redactional poetry. Second, the observation concerning the "personal" tone of the "confessions" begs the question, as has been shown above.[8] Third, the claim that comparison of Jeremiah 2–3 and Jeremiah 30–31 reveals a development in style from short sayings to extended poem misrepresents the structure of Jeremiah 2–3, itself now commonly recognized as an extended composition. Fourth, as will be discussed below, the conclusion that Jeremiah 2–3 and 30–31 embody Jeremiah's early preaching to the former Northern kingdom owes more to external assumptions concerning the chronology of Jeremiah's career than to internal evidence. According to the standard chronology, Jeremiah

---

[7]*Der Prophet Jeremia: Leben und Werk*, Urban-Taschenbücher 416 (Stuttgart: Kohlhammer, 1993).

[8]See above, 15-44.

began preaching decades before the Babylonian crisis. On the assumption that some deposit of that early preaching must have been left in the book, Seybold (along with many others) equates early preaching with the beginning of the book.

Nevertheless, the style of Jeremiah 2–10 does not differ significantly from the poetry of 11–20. The tone of Jeremiah 2–6 is no more optimistic than the tone of Jeremiah 7–10 or 11–20. The early portions of the book address Judah and Jerusalem and they refer to "Israel" either for purposes of generalizing the message or in historical comparison in the context of the Babylonian crisis.[9] The pan-Israel emphasis, notable especially in relation to certain headings in Jeremiah 2–3 and in the appeal to the Exodus tradition, presents a particularly vexing—though apparently as yet unrecognized—challenge to scholars insistent on the view that Jeremiah 2–3 represent the prophet's early preaching to the former Northern kingdom ("Israel"). In a recent article, D. Böhler[10] objects to the analysis offered by M. Biddle who distinguishes between masculine address to all Israel in all generations and feminine address to Lady Jerusalem.[11] Böhler suggests that alternation in gender and number of forms of address in Jeremiah 2–3 need not be seen as alternation in addressees. The entirety of Jeremiah 2–3 addresses the former Northern Kingdom, in Böhler's view. Masculine forms of address refer to Israel as an organized political entity, "Israel in the land"; feminine forms refer to

---

[9]See, e.g., R. Liwak, *Der Prophet und die Geschichte: eine literar-historische Untersuchung zum Jeremiabuch*, BWANT 121 (Stuttgart: Kohlhammer, 1987) concerning Jeremiah 2–6 as a collection of materials from throughout Jeremiah's career; C. Levin, "Noch einmal: Die Anfänge des Propheten Jeremia," *VT* 31 (1981): 428-40 and E. Ruprecht, "Ist die Berufung Jeremias "im Jünglingsalter" und seine "Frühverkündigung" eine theologische Konstruktion der deuteronomistischen Redaktion des Jeremiabuches?" in *Schöpfung und Befreiung: Für Claus Westermann zum 80. Geburtstag*, R. Albertz, et al., eds. (Stuttgart: Calwer Verlag, 1989) 79-103, concerning the programmatic tendencies of the narrative of Jeremiah's call; and Biddle, *Redaction*, 132-34, concerning the pan-Israel interests of Jeremiah 2–3.

[10]"Geschlechterdifferenz und Landbesitz: Strukturuntersuchungen zu Jer 2,2–4,2," in *Jeremia und die "deuteronomistische Bewegung,"* 91-127.

[11]*Redaction*, 33-38.

a "landless woman," without independent means of subsistence.[12] The disagreement between Biddle and Böhler illustrates clearly the significance of careful attention to the identification and characterization of voices (and addressees) in prophetic literature.

The debate hinges on four key points. First, Böhler regards gender and number largely as grammatical features while the method employed in the current study regards them as potentially significant literary clues to characterization.[13] The feminine addressee in Jeremiah 2–3 is unspecified. Presumably the author (whether Jeremiah or a redactor) had some figure in mind. Who? Governed by the assumption that Jeremiah 2–3 represent Jeremiah's early preaching, Böhler argues that "she" is none other than "they" (masc., in other words the Ephraimites). Biddle asks whether this feminine figure has contact with any poetic phenomena elsewhere in the book, in the Hebrew Bible, or in Ancient Near Eastern literature. In point of fact, several texts in Jeremiah employ the same personification with very similar lexical and thematic features in reference to the explicitly identified "Lady Jerusalem."[14] Furthermore, the feminine personification of "Mother" Jerusalem and other "Mother" capital cities is common in the Hebrew Bible[15] and seems related to a common ancient Near Eastern metaphor.[16] Böhler, however, overlooks these affinities as

---

[12]Böhler, "Geschlechterdifferenz," 109.

[13]As in Biddle, *Redaction*.

[14]Jer 4:14; 6:18; 13:25-27; 15:5-9; cf. 4:18, 30; 5:7; 13:20-22; 22:20-23; see *Redaction*, 68-71 and chap. 2 above, 20-22.

[15]Jer 50:2-3, 22-27; 51:41-46; Lam 1:2, 5, 8-9, 19; Psa 48:1-3, 12-13; Isa 47:1-15; 49:14-21; 50:1-3, and often; Ezek 16; 25:7, and often; Nah 3; etc.

[16]See M. Biddle, "The Figure of Lady Jerusalem: Identification, Deification and Personification of Cities in the Ancient Near East" in *The Canon in Comparative Perspective*, ed. B. Batto, W. Hallo and K. L. Younger, Scripture in Context 4 (Lewiston NY: Edwin Mellen Press, 1991) 173-94 and literature cited there; see also K. Jeppesen, "Mother Zion, Father Servant: A Reading of Isaiah 49-55," *Of Prophets' Visions and the Wisdom of Sages: Essays in Honour of R. Norman Whybray on his Seventieth Birthday*, ed. H. McKay and D. Clines, JSOTSup 162 (Sheffield: Sheffield, 1993); M. Turner, "Daughter Zion: Lament and Restoration" (diss., Emory University, 1992); F. Dobbs-Allsop, *Weep, O Daughter of Zion: A Study of the City-Lament Genre in the Hebrew Bible* (Rome: Pontifical Biblical Institute Press, 1993); K. Darr, *Isaiah's Vision and the*

well as those between the "Jerusalem" material in Jeremiah 2 and the treatment of Jerusalem's "wilderness" origins in Ezekiel 16.[17]

Second, Böhler and others who insist that Jeremiah 2–3 address Ephraim fail to adequately explain the address to "all the families of the house of Israel" (2:4) whom YHWH "brought up from the land of Egypt" (2:6) or to the "Israel" of the wilderness (2:3) who was not a "homeborn slave" (2:14). Does the phrase "all the families" refer to the ten Northern tribes only? Did Ephraim "wander in the wilderness" alone? Was Ephraim alone freed from Egyptian slavery? No evidence whatsoever contradicts the conclusion that "Israel" in Jeremiah 2–3 (with the exception of the insertion 3:6-11) ever refers to any entity other than pan-Israel. Should Jer 10:1 or 18:6 be assigned to Jeremiah's early pro-Samarian period? How does one account for the fact that the book of Ezekiel regularly uses the phrase "house of Israel" to designate Judah only[18] or that Deutero-Isaiah also regularly employs Israel for the Judean exiles? Judean prophets in the sixth century apparently considered "Israel" or "house of Israel" an appropriate designation for Southerners, as well. What evidence requires the conclusion that Jeremiah used the term in the older, political sense in Jeremiah 2–6?

Third, Böhler reads certain passages with a rigid historicism. He insists, for example, that וְעַתָּה in Jer 2:18 be translated as a temporal[19] and that the waw in v 18b be translated "and,"[20] so that this verse must refer to a moment in Ephraim's history when diplomatic overtures were made toward *both* Egypt and Assyria. Other translations are certainly possible, especially in light of the sophisticated literary activity which produced the final form of the text.[21]

Family of God, Literary Currents in Biblical Interpretation (Louisville: Westminster/John Knox Press, 1994); and P. Willey, "The Servant of YHWH and Daughter Zion: Alternating visions of YHWH's Community," SBLSP 1995 (forthcoming).

[17]"Geschlechterdifferenz," 92n.6: "Did Jerusalem wander in the wilderness?"; cf. 105n.38. See, however, J. Galambush, *Jerusalem in the Book of Ezekiel: The City as Yahweh's Wife*, SBLDS 130 (Atlanta: Scholars Press, 1992) esp. 89-109.

[18]Ezek 3:1,4,7; 4:3; 6:11, etc.

[19]"Geschlechterdifferenz," 93n.7.

[20]Ibid., 122n.94.

[21]"And now," understood as a rhetorical device, cf. BDB 774a; "or," cf. Carroll, *Jeremiah*, 127, and Holladay, *Jeremiah*, 52.

Finally, Böhler seems unconcerned with redactional processes. He excises texts which do not support his thesis[22] and prefers LXX, as a rule (2:1-2), except when it challenges his thesis.[23] One wonders whether Böhler can sustain his argument that redactors can be expected to have produced seamless compositions in the face of considerable evidence to the contrary.[24]

Scholars seem to show interest in a chronological arrangement of the book, in part, because of an assumption that Jeremiah must have once been optimistic about the possibility of repentance. As it stands, however, the book offers little or no clear indications of the nature of Jeremiah's preaching of repentance. The overarching contention of the canonical book of Jeremiah is that YHWH had *already* determined Judah's fate *before* Jeremiah ever began preaching. This contention has affected the *shape* of the book to the extent that, if Jeremiah ever entertained significant hope that the YHWH's anger could be assuaged, evidence for this attitude has been virtually effaced. It remains for interpretation to deal not with questions of *ipsissima verba*, but of fidelity to existing voices in the text.

Understanding this whole constellation of problems can be significantly advanced through precise analysis of materials that refer to "intercession," "repentance," "confession," and "mourning/lament." Too often, interpreters treat these modes of expression as a conglomerate, understanding mourning/lament as a form of intercession, almost automatically assuming that statements of prophetic pain imply disappointment in the failure of intercession or that statements of divine pain equate with statements of prophetic pain. In particular, careful attention to YHWH's prohibitions against prophetic intercession and a reassessment of the role of intercession in the canonical function of the confessions render it no longer possible to see the confessions as the product of prophetic disappointment. Instead, they shift the locus of attention to the question of YHWH's role as judge.

---

[22]2:28c which refers to Judah.

[23]LXX omits "in the wilderness in the land not sown," 2:2.

[24]"Geschlechterdifferenz," 92n.6. What would he make of Genesis 1–2; Exodus 19–21; Isaiah 2–4; and Hosea 1–3, to cite only a few obvious examples?

In this regard, finally, the prose superstructure of the book is not consistent on the question of the criteria YHWH employs when deciding to punish. The majority of texts insist that YHWH had already reached a decision concerning Judah's fate as early as the reign of Manasseh (Jer 15:1-4). A few others, however, suggest that YHWH's verdicts are always contingent (Jer 18:5-11). The confessions question whether YHWH, in fact, punishes the evil and whether divine justice can distinguish the few righteous among the many who are evil.

An Analysis of the Concept of Prophetic Intercession

The question of Jeremiah's intercessory activity and God's attitude toward it is much more complicated than is often recognized. The prohibitions against intercession that occur beginning in Jeremiah 7 (Jer 7:16; 11:14; 14:11; 16:5-9; compare 15:1) seem to prohibit an activity that Jeremiah 7–20 does not portray, and thus they raise the issues of prophetic disobedience and the role of the prophetic confessions. Researchers frequently interpret this prohibition in relation to the individualistic orientation of the confessions, arguing that Jeremiah 11–20 depicts the prophet's retreat to private appeal to YHWH since he is forbidden to intercede for the people.[25] While productive for a reading of the confessions in terms of a spiritual portrait of the prophet, this interpretation fails to account for the occurrence of the prohibition against intercession in Jer 7:16-20. Many scholars interested in a spiritual portrait of the prophet, both those who would regard such a portrait as historically reliable and those who would consider it a literary product, focus considerable attention on several passages in Jeremiah 8–10 thought to reflect the inner struggles of the prophet charged with condemning a people with whom he identifies (for example, 8:18–9:2). Since, however, Jeremiah 8–10 does not contain prophetic intercession,[26] and since Jeremiah 7–10 does

---

[25]Cf. C. Seitz, "The Prophet Moses," 10: "an avenue of discourse is cut off for the prophet. He can no longer intercede on behalf of the people. This fact, and the restriction of the prophetic word to judgement (20,8), gives rise to persecution and challenge on the horizontal plane. The loss of the intercessory role, in its social dimension, gives rise to the intercessions of the prophet, as individual, on his own behalf."

[26]See above, 28-32.

not depict the prophet as disobedient to the prohibition against intercession, the prohibition in Jeremiah 7 must participate in a conversation which does not relate primarily to any prayers of Jeremiah on the behalf of his people.

"Intercession" in Jeremiah

Fourteen texts in the book seem to refer, directly or indirectly, to prophetic intercession. In addition to the four texts in Jeremiah 7–20 that prohibit intercession, eight others report or seem to report Jeremiah's intercession on behalf of the people or some component of the people. One of these texts (18:20) appears to refer to Jeremiah's request that YHWH remember that he has interceded on behalf of his people; in another very similar passage (17:16) the prophet defends his preaching on the grounds that he has only spoken the message given him. Six other prose texts relate to Jeremiah's willingness to mediate between YHWH and the king or a Judean group concerning questions of YHWH's will. Three texts (21:2; 37:3,7) involve Jeremiah's response to Zedekiah's request that the prophet seek YHWH's answer to the king's question. These two accounts bear remarkable similarities to one another and may, in fact, represent a doublet.[27] The first account is markedly pro*golah* (Babylonian), while the second is proremnant (Judean) and antirefugee (Egyptian). Three others (42:2,4,20) involve Jeremiah's similar response to the request of the Judean group interested in fleeing to Egypt. This group of texts may represent the stances of progolah and proremnant elements of the tradition.[28] In any case, none of these texts seems concerned with Jeremiah's freedom to mediate between God and his people.

Three other texts are each unique. In the MT of Jer 15:11, a key passage for understanding the "confessions" and a very difficult passage textually,[29] YHWH reminds Jeremiah that he has "interceded" in Jeremi-

---

[27]See W. Thiel, *Redaktion*, 231. Contrast W. McKane, 492-94.

[28]See K.-F. Pohlmann, *Studien zum Jeremiabuch: Ein Beitrag zur Frage nach der Entstehung des Jeremiabuches*, FRLANT 118 (Göttingen: Vandenhoeck & Ruprecht, 1978).

[29]See W. McKane, 347-49; R. Carroll, *Jeremiah*, 325; D. Bak, 134. The confusion with regard to the identity of the speaker regularly encountered in the textual tradition of Jeremiah appears here, as well. LXX seems to have read a form of אמן instead of MT's אמר. LXX has Jeremiah protest that he has faithfully

ah's life for the prophet's good. In Jer 27:18 Jeremiah taunts the prophets of peace with the challenge that they prove their authenticity by interceding with YHWH to prevent the plundering of Jerusalem and the temple. Finally, in Jeremiah 29:7, the prophet advises the Babylonian deportees to pray to YHWH on behalf of Babylon, since their welfare will henceforth be inextricably bound with that of their captors.

---

interceded with YHWH on behalf of his (Jeremiah's?) enemies. The two subsequent verbs present further difficulties. MT's שֵׁרוֹתִךָ appears to be corrupt (note *Kethib/Qere*) with possible derivations from the roots שׁרה, "to let loose," ("I set you free") and שׁרר, "to be firm, strong" ("I give you strength"); LXX has κατευ-θυνόντων αὐτῶν, "setting them right, guiding them." The final verb, פגע, "to intercede," presents difficulties of a different nature. How can YHWH be described as "interceding" on the prophet's behalf with his enemies? In MT's version, 15:11 parallels the thought and language of 15:20 so that the entire section serves as YHWH's charge to the prophet to stand up to the difficulties of preaching an unpopular message. YHWH's intercession (perhaps "intervention" would be a better translation) takes the form of YHWH's presence to save and deliver (15:20). If Jeremiah will "return," he will be permitted to "stand before" YHWH (15:19) as the bronze wall which cannot be broken (15:12, 20).

Interestingly, the tendencies of MT and LXX at this point conform to characteristics of the two versions identified by A. Diamond ("Jeremiah's Confessions in the LXX and MT: A Witness to Developing Canonical Function," *VT* 60 [1990]: 33-50). Diamond's analysis centers around instances in which LXX "effaces prophetically specific readings" (45), especially by "[exploiting] generic connections to cultic lament" (46). Leaving aside questions of priority raised by Diamond's choice of verbs (LXX "effaces" MT or MT "elaborates" LXX?), the MT of Jer 15:11 obscures to a degree the identity of YHWH's dialogue partner. The sequence of a lament over Mother Jerusalem (15:5-9), a personal lament in which the lamenter apostrophizes his own "mother," and a judgment oracle (15:13-14) not easily understood as addressed to Jeremiah predisposes a reader to expect the addressee here to be some collective representative of the people. Similarly, references to the "enemies" in MT seem to have the enemies of the nation in view, not Jeremiah's personal antagonists. Of course, when the text reaches 15:19-21, in both MT and LXX these obscurities seem to have been resolved in favor of the individual prophetic figure and his personal enemies. At any rate, one may not confidently employ Jer 15:11 as evidence either for the intercessory activity of the prophet Jeremiah or for the literary depiction of such a motif.

"Mediation"

In terms of pertinence to the issue at hand, most of these texts can be discarded straightway. Some do not refer to Jeremiah's activity (15:11; 27:18; 29:7) and others refer less to "intercession," precisely understood, than to "intermediation" (21:2; 37:3, 7; 42:2, 4, 20).[30] Texts in the second group do not describe Jeremiah's partisan activity—he neither represents the interests of those for whom he speaks nor pleads their case with YHWH—but a more neutral messenger function. The people or the king wish to know something from YHWH; Jeremiah asks and reports the answer.

Jeremiah 17:16 and 18:20 remain the best candidates for unmistakable references to Jeremiah's intercessory activity. Closer examination, however, suggests that neither provides support for the traditional view of Jeremiah's struggle with his failure to effect Judah's repentance and YHWH's forgiveness.

Although, once again, the text of Jer 17:16 presents serious difficulties,[31] it clearly describes the speaker's disappointment, not with failed

---

[30]S. Balentine ("The Prophet as Intercessor: A Reassessment," *JBL* 103 [1984]: 161-73) points out the temptation to describe any and all prophetic speech directed to God as "intercession." As he defines it, intercession "begins at the point when one addresses God on behalf of the concerns of someone else" (162). Although Balentine's definition implies as much, an additional criterion characteristic of "intercession" should also be explicitly stated: Intercession involves an effort to influence a decision. The six instances of "intermediation" in Jeremiah involve what Balentine terms "prophetic inquiries." In such inquiries, often signalled by the occurrence of the term דָּרַשׁ (21:2; 37:7), the prophet serves merely as the go-between who "is asked to deliver God's word for the particular situation involved." This function does not require the compassionate, sympathetic involvement of the prophet in the lives of those he represents; it certainly cannot be described in terms of the prophet's "identification" with his people. The model for such "intermediation" is not Moses begging God to pardon his people (Exod 32:11-14) but Samuel telling Saul where to find the lost donkeys (1 Sam 10).

[31]The initial phrase is very difficult. The verb אוץ can mean "to urge" (Gen 19:15; Exod 5:13), "to be narrow" (Josh 17:15), "to hurry" (Josh 10:13), or "to labor (to the point of weariness)" (Isa 22:4). The complement מֵרֹעֶה complicates the translator's decision. As pointed in MT, it seems to be a form of the

expectations of repentance, but with the delay of announced punishment. "They" taunt him that YHWH's word remains, as yet, unrealized (v 15). He counters that punishment is not his idea; he has only proclaimed that which YHWH has planned (v 16). YHWH must make good this threat; YHWH must not allow YHWH's servant to be ashamed.

Commentators almost universally interpret Jer 18:20 in relation to the traditional view of Jeremiah as intercessor.[32] Indeed, this verse refers twice to the "good" Jeremiah has done the people, specifying the nature of that good as an effort to "turn [YHWH's] wrath from them."

עמד לפני—"to stand before"

The key phrase זְכֹר עָמְדִי לְפָנֶיךָ strongly suggests another possibility, however. Usually understood as the prophet's call for YHWH to remember that, like Abraham (Gen 18:22) he has interceded on the behalf of others, the predominant usage of the phrase in the Hebrew Bible relates to service rendered to a superior. Apart from the use in the sense of "to stand up to someone, to withstand someone," common especially in military contexts (Exod 9:11; 1 Sam 6:20; 2 Kgs 10:4; Nah 1:6; Psa

---

root associated with "shepherding" and "pasturing." Many commentators suggest repointing to a form of the root רעה, "evil." Finally, אֱנוּשׁ may be pointed with MT to mean "weakness, illness, disaster" or, alternatively, as the common noun "man." LXX understands the verb in the latter sense, its complement as "evil," and the noun as "man." It renders, "I have not grown weary (> κοπιάω) following you; I have not sought the day of man." Although no sure solution seems possible, the first clause can be expected to parallel the second in meaning. The first verb, then, can be expected to parallel the second, "I have not desired," an expectation which suggests the meaning "to urge." Similarly, the complements אֱנוּשׁ and מֵרֹעֶה can be expected to parallel one another. The best solution for this equation seems to be "evil" and "disaster." The only remaining difficulty is the force of "after you" in the first clause. RSV's translation offers the best sense: "I have not pressed thee to send evil, nor have I desired the day of disaster. . . . "

[32]Although it does not relate directly to the issue under consideration, the text of Jer 18:20 differs in MT and LXX once again in a manner consistent with the contrasting treatments the two versions give texts which deal with the image of the prophet. LXX does not translate the phrase "for they have dug a pit for my life." Instead, it offers, "because they have spoken words against my soul and their correction is hidden from me."

76:8; 147:17; Prov 27:4; Dan 8:4,7; Ezra 9:15), and a few unique usages,[33] all other occurrences describe circumstances involving the appearance of an individual or a group before a superior—most often the king, a royal official, or the deity—in order to render service, receive instructions, or submit to the superior's authority. The image seems to suggest standing in waiting before the seated superior. A few examples will illustrate this usage.

Let a young maiden be sought for my lord the king, and let her stand before (RSV "wait upon") the king.   (1 Kgs 1:2)

Happy are these your servants, who continually stand before you [Solomon] and hear your wisdom.   (1 Kgs 10:8 = 2 Chron 9:7)

But he forsook the counsel which the old men gave him, and took counsel with the young men who had grown up with him and stood before him.
                    (1 Kgs 12:8 = 2 Chron 10:8; cf. 1 Kgs 12:6 = 2 Chron 10:5)

By extension, the claim that "one stands before someone" equates with a claim "to be in someone's service," "to represent someone." Joseph is thirty when he comes to "stand before Pharaoh" and to represent him throughout Egypt (Gen 41:46). YHWH refers to Joshua's service to Moses (Deut 1:38). The prophets Elijah and Elisha frequently identify themselves as YHWH's servants with a version of the statement, "As YHWH the God of Israel lives, before whom I stand " (1 Kgs 17:1; cf. 1 Kgs 18:15; 2 Kgs 3:14; 5:16 [RSV translates the last two occurrences, "whom I serve"]; see also 1 Kgs 19:11). Young David comes to "stand before" King Saul as court musician (1 Sam 16:21, 22). Daniel spends three years training before joining those who "stand before the king" (Dan 1:5, 19; 2:2). In the heavenly court, heavenly beings make themselves available to divine commission by "standing before" YHWH (1 Kgs 22:21 = 2 Chron 18:20). The phrase often refers, similarly, to priests who

---

[33]Exod 17:6 refers to YHWH "standing before" Moses; in Lev 18:23 the phrase describes sexual activity; Dan 8:3,6 employ it to mean simply "to be situated."

minister in YHWH's service (Num 27:21; Deut 10:8; 18:7; Ezek 44:15; 2 Chron 29:11; cf. 1 Kgs 8:22 = 2 Chron 6:12; Zech 3:1, 3, 4).[34]

A second functional realm involves "standing before" a superior in order to transact business (Gen 43:15) or to seek the superior's decision with regard, especially, to some legal matter. These cases imply the superior's responsibility for administering justice. Since this application of the phrase most closely approaches "intercession," each instance will be cited.

Abraham still stood before YHWH. Then Abraham approached, and said, " . . . Shall not the Judge of all the earth do right?"   (Gen 18:22-25)

Then YHWH said to Moses, "Rise early in the morning and stand before Pharaoh, and say to him, Thus says YHWH, the God of the Hebrews, 'Let my people go.' "   (Exod 9:13; cf. 9:10)

And [the daughters of Zelophehad] stood before Moses, and before Eleazar the priest, and before the leaders and all the congregation at the door of the tent of meeting, and said, " . . . Give us an inheritance among our father's family."   (Num 27:2,4)

The cities shall be for you a refuge from the avenger, that the manslayer may not die until he stands before the congregation for judgment.
          (Num 35:12; see also Josh 20:6, 9)

Then two harlots came to the king, and stood before him [to present their case for judgment].   (1 Kgs 3:16)

---

[34]Balentine ("Prophet as Intercessor," 166) emphasizes this use of the phrase in regard to priests who represent YHWH to the people rather than interceding with YHWH on the people's behalf. Relatedly, the phrase also occurs in reference to the congregation's service to God in worship. They, too, "stand before YHWH" on occasions when YHWH's presence is expected (Lev 9:5; Deut 4:10). Kings, especially Solomon, occasionally "stand before" YHWH or the ark, the symbol of YHWH's presence, to perform priestly functions (1 Kgs 3:15; 8:22). Balentine (n. 18) calls attention to the expression, "stand in the breach" (עָמַד בַּפֶּרֶץ), as the more specific term for (prophetic) intercession (Ezek 22:30; cf. 13:5; Psa 106:23).

> So Hazael went to meet [Elisha]. . . . When he came and stood before him, he said, "Your son Benhadad, king of Syria, has sent me to you, saying, 'Shall I recover?'" (2 Kgs 8:9)

> And Esther rose and stood before the king. And she said, "If it please the king. . . . " (Esth 8:4)

Notably, only two of these texts (Gen 18:22-25; Esth 8:4) involve the notion of interceding on the behalf of others. Typically, someone comes "to stand before" a superior in order to present one's own case (sometimes as a representative of a group to which one belongs, as in Esther). Significantly, these pleas do not seek mercy. Instead, supplicants appeal to superiors as the administrators of justice: Even the well-known example of Abraham's "intercessory prayer" focuses around arguments based upon YHWH's status as "Judge of All the Earth" and seems concerned primarily with YHWH's character and reputation for justice. Abraham does not seek an opportunity for the unrighteous in Sodom and Gomorrah to repent nor does he call upon YHWH to exercise mercy. In this regard, Abraham functions less as an "intercessor" representing the interests of the inhabitants of Sodom and Gomorrah and more as YHWH's servant protecting YHWH's reputation for justice.

In sum, then, the phrase עמד לפני does not seem to be associated with the concept of intercession. Instead, it refers to direct access to a superior (especially the king or the deity). In turn, this access implies either that one stands in the service of the superior or that one approaches the superior to invoke the superior's jurisdiction over a particular matter.

עמד לפני in Jeremiah

Seven of the nine occurrences of the phrase in Jeremiah fall rather straightforwardly into two of the categories outlined above. The doublet concerning the fate of foreign rulers (49:19 = 50:44) describes their inability to "withstand" YHWH's onslaught. Five other texts scattered throughout the book refer to "serving" YHWH (7:10; 15:19; 35:19) or an earthly ruler (40:10; 52:12). Interestingly, the parallel to Jer 52:12 in 2 Kgs 25:8 employs a form of עבד instead of Jeremiah's עמד, a variant easily explained as confusion of ב and מ, a confusion facilitated, no doubt, by the synonymy of the two expressions.

The two remaining occurrences (15:1; 18:20) have been traditionally understood as references to Jeremiah's intercessory activity. The context of Jer 15:1 provides very little information concerning the character of the activity of Moses and Samuel envisioned in this text, however. Does the text refer to their reputations as representatives of the people (intercessors), as spokespersons for YHWH (repentance preachers), or as servants of YHWH particularly interested in protecting YHWH's reputation for justice (compare Genesis 18)?[35] Does the comparison to Moses and Samuel suggest that even Moses would have found no basis for appealing to YHWH's justice and fidelity to his promise (Exod 32:12-13 and Jer 15:4; compare Jer 14:7,21)?

On the other hand, the context of Jer 18:20 offers several clues as to how the phrase should be understood there. The so-called "alternative sermon"[36] (18:6-12) establishes the tone for subsequent material in terms of the choice YHWH places before the people through the prophet's preaching. Jeremiah, speaking for YHWH, offers them good (טוֹבָה) if they repent or evil (רָעָה) if they persist in their wrongdoing. The people, however, stubbornly and rebelliously insist on continuing their current behavior, in effect refusing YHWH's offer (18:12). Indeed, in the immediate context (18:18) of the prophetic complaint (18:19-23), the people express a desire to silence Jeremiah and end his preaching of repentance. This expression of intent elicits Jeremiah's charge that he has only represented YHWH (עמד לפני) and spoken "concerning them good" or "for their benefit."

---

[35]Neither of these figures enjoyed unmitigated success as "intercessors" according to canonical tradition. Just as Abraham before them succeeded "only" in gaining the safety of Lot and his family, Moses (Exodus 32) succeeded in reminding YHWH of the promise to the patriarchs although the entire generation of those involved in the golden calf episode were punished for their sin. Samuel's efforts in relation to the choice of the king and, especially, in relation to first king, himself, were total "failures." Both of them "stood before YHWH" most effectively as spokespersons proclaiming the divine will.

[36]For discussions of this genre and assessments of its relationship to the source and redaction problems of the book of Jeremiah, see S. Herrmann, *Die prophetischen Heilserwartungen im Alten Testament: Ursprung und Gestaltwandel*, BWANT 85 (Stuttgart: Kohlhammer, 1965) 162-65; W. Thiel, *Redaktion*, 214-18; and H. Weippert, *Die Prosareden des Jeremiabuches*, BZAW 132 (New York: de Gruyter, 1973) 50-67.

How has Jeremiah spoken for their benefit? The traditional response has been that he interceded on their behalf, seeking YHWH's mercy. The context suggests, however, and the syntax of v 20 permits,[37] a reference to Jeremiah's admonitions to repent and warnings of the consequences of failure to do so. As YHWH's representative, he described the alternatives in an effort "to avert [YHWH's] wrath," that is, he spoke "to their benefit." This understanding also helps to explain what would otherwise be Jeremiah's radical shift from a willingness to plead for YHWH's mercy on the people to a vindictive anger because of personal injustice (vv 21-23). Jeremiah's enemies deserve the fate he wishes upon them not because they have failed to appreciate his tender compassion for them, but because they have rejected the word of YHWH (v 18), and, ultimately, YHWH himself (vv 12-17).

Analysis of the Prohibition against Intercession in Jeremiah 7–20: Divine Discourse

Given the fact, then, that Jeremiah 7–20 does not describe an active intercessory role for Jeremiah and that Jeremiah 21–45 reports the prophet's active involvement as a substantially neutral spokesperson-intermediary, the few texts which prohibit the prophet from interceding voice a unique concern. Working on the hypothesis that the book of Jeremiah portrays the prophet as YHWH's mouthpiece (not as the people's representative), the intention of YHWH's prohibitions against intercession can be expected to relate to some theme other than Jeremiah's sympathy for his people.

A careful exegesis of the prohibitions and their contexts (7:1-28; 11:1-14; 14:1–16:13) reveals the dominance of YHWH's voice in the dialogue between the deity and the prophet. These texts explain the futility

---

[37]The text here is relatively certain and the Hebrew is relatively simple, but the proper translation is far from assured. In addition to the question of the connotations of "to stand before," the (notoriously evasive) preposition עַל presents its own difficulties; and the mechanism by which Jeremiah's "speaking" is intended to "avert [YHWH's] wrath" is not immediately clear. Many commentators resolve this matrix of difficulties as W. McKane (*Jeremiah*, 435) does when he translates: "Is good to be repaid with evil? Remember how I stood in your presence to make a plea on their behalf, to avert your anger from them."

of intercession on the basis of YHWH's determination to punish a people whose unwillingness to repent compounds a long history of idolatry, disobedience, and susceptibility to false prophecy.

Jeremiah 7:1-28

A striking feature of Jeremiah 1-19 in the final form of the text involves the framing of virtually every section of material as dialogue between YHWH and the prophet.[38] As the text stands, it seems to depict an extended series of revelatory events. While it can be assumed that Jeremiah must have executed YHWH's instructions (for example, to "stand in the gate of YHWH's house," 7:1), no text prior to Jer 19:14 explicitly records that Jeremiah appeared publicly. Furthermore, the incipits which portray the text as private revelation introduce a third voice, that of the anonymous narrator or redactor.[39] Awareness of the formation history of the book, however, does not permit the interpreter simply to set aside the

---

[38]The standard pattern in Jeremiah 1–19 involves a unit heading specifying the following as YHWH's communication to the prophet (Jer 1:4, 11, 12, 14; 3:6; 11:6, 9; 13:1, 8; 14:1, 11; 15:1; 16:1; 18:1, 5) and sometimes including instructions for the subsequent delivery of the content to the people (Jer 2:1-2; 3:11-12; 7:1-2; 8:4; 11:1-3; 13:12; 14:17; 16:10; 17:19-20; 19:1-3, 10). The few exceptions (Jer 4:5; 5:20; 10:1) to the pattern differ only in that they do not provide details concerning the revelation of the divine word to the prophet. They, too, fail to indicate whether, when, and where Jeremiah actually delivered these messages. The first passage in the book which reports Jeremiah's *actual* behavior in the public realm occurs in Jer 19:14. Beginning with Jer 20:1, the normal pattern involves reports of Jeremiah's public behavior itself.

[39]On the basis of his analysis of the phenomenon of "nested" introductory formulas, H. Van Dyke Parunak distinguishes between three "communication events": committal, delivery, and report ("Some Discourse Functions of Prophetic Quotation Formulas in Jeremiah," in *Biblical Hebrew and Discourse Linguistics*, ed. R. Bergen [Dallas: Summer Institute of Linguistics, 1994] 493). Parunak's analysis can be expanded to include private communications from deity to prophet (Parunak's "background" category, information relayed from the deity to the prophet as part of the "committal" phase, information against which the subsequent oracle is to be understood, does not include communications to the prophet which were not intended in relation to oracles for public delivery; see 497) and reported or projected speech within oracles. Again, Jeremiah 1–19 does not, in fact, report the delivery of oracles.

narrative structure of the text. Rather, this structure constitutes the over-arching "voice" of the text in its final form. By implication, this voice suggests that from the outset YHWH imparts substantial information con-cerning the full scope of his intentions for Judah prior to Jeremiah's initial public appearance. This emphasis upon the divine word produces a very complicated discourse structure.

Narrator
   [1]The word which was to Jeremiah from YHWH, saying:[40]

   YHWH (to Jeremiah)
      [2]"Stand in the gate of the YHWH's temple
         and proclaim there this word and say,

      "Jeremiah" (as posited by YHWH)
         'Hear the word of YHWH all Judah
            which enters these gates to worship YHWH!
         [3]Thus says YHWH Sebaoth, God of Israel:[41]

---

[40]H. Parunak (499) classifies headings such as Jer 7:1 as "incipits," which "sometimes seems to govern collections of oracles rather than single oracles, thus providing a higher level of grouping in the structure of the book." The extent of the collection governed by 7:1 is difficult to determine. It clearly subsumes vv 1-28. The sudden shift to 2fs address in v 29 may mark a new beginning; alternatively, the continuation of 3pl forms in 7:30–8:4 ("You shall say to them") may indicate that the continuation of YHWH's speech *to* Jeremiah *about* the Judeans and 7:29 may be "reported" speech embedded within the extended context. The next unmistakable "incipit" occurs in Jer 10:1. The hypothesis that Jer 7:1 intends to define the entirety of Jer 7–10 as YHWH-speech finds support in the interpretation of individual laments within this section as YHWH speech (see above, 28-40).

[41]LXX preserves a much shorter introduction resulting in a much simpler dialogical structure. Instead of MT's complicated, multilayered citations, LXX reads "Hear the work of the Lord, all Judah, Thus says the Lord, the God of Israel, 'Correct your ways. . . . '" Jeremiah scholarship is moving toward a consensus in view of mounting evidence that LXX and MT of Jeremiah represent two editions of the book. In cases such as Jer 7:1-2, then, classical text-critical issues do not strictly apply. Instead, Jer 7:1-2 MT exemplifies an overall trend in the MT edition of the book toward a consistent framing of the prophetic word, understood in the broadest sense as the text of the book of Jeremiah as the word

"YHWH" (as cited by theoretical "Jeremiah")
      "Correct your ways and your deeds
            and I will dwell with you in this place.
[4]Do not entrust yourselves to false words, saying,

People (as posited by YHWH,
according to "Jeremiah" as posited by YHWH)
            'YHWH's temple, YHWH's temple,
                  YHWH's temple are these.'

[5]"Indeed, if you truly correct your ways and your deeds, if you truly do justice one toward the other, [6]if you do not oppress the alien, the orphan, and the widow, and if you do not shed innocent blood in this place, and if you do not follow after other gods to your own hurt, [7]then I will dwell with you in this place in the land which I gave to your fathers in perpetuity.

[8]"Look, you entrust yourselves to false words, to no avail! [9]Will you commit adultery, kill, steal, swear falsely, burn incense to Baal, and follow after other gods whom you do not know [10]and then come and stand before me in this house called by my name and say,
      'We are saved!'
in order to (continue) do(ing) all these abominations? [11]Has this house, called by my name, become a den of thieves in your eyes? Look, I have seen it myself!"
—an utterance of YHWH—

[12]"Go now to my place in Shiloh where I caused my name to dwell before and see what I did to it because of the evil of my people Israel. [13]And now, because you did all these deeds"
—an utterance of YHWH—
      "although I warned you (I warned persistently) and you neither heard nor responded, [14]I will do to this house called by my name in which you trust and to the place which I gave to you

---

of YHWH (cf. MT's treatment of divine laments in Jeremiah 8–9, e.g., in contrast to LXX). Jeremiah 11:1-3 indicate, however, that LXX could frame texts in the same manner. The difference is one of degree and consistency in the execution of an editorial tendency.

and your fathers just as I did to Shiloh. [15]And I will cast you away from me just as I cast away your brothers all the seed of Ephraim."

[16]"So you (Jeremiah), do not pray for this people, and do not lift up a lament or a prayer for them, and do not intercede with me, because I will not listen to you. [17]Can your eyes not see what they do in the cities of Judah and in the streets of Jerusalem? [18]The children gather wood, the fathers light the fire, the women knead dough to make cakes for the Queen of Heaven, and they pour our libations to other gods in order to provoke me. [19]Do they provoke me?"
—an utterance of YHWH—
"and not themselves to their own shame?"

[20]Therefore thus says the Lord YHWH:
"Look! My anger and my wrath will be poured out on this place—on people, on beasts, on trees of the field, and on fruits of the ground—and it will burn and not be quenched."

"Jeremiah" (as posited by YHWH)
[21]Thus says YHWH Sebaoth, the God of Israel:

"YHWH" (as cited by theoretical "Jeremiah")
"Add your burnt offerings to your sacrifices and eat meat. [22]But I did not tell your fathers and I did not command them on the day when I[42] brought them from the land of Egypt concerning matters of offering and sacrifice. [23]But with this word I commanded them, saying,

"YHWH" (embedded within speech of "YHWH"
as cited by theoretical "Jeremiah")
'Hear my voice and I will be your God and you will be my people and walk in all the ways I command you in order that it may be well with you.'

[24]"But they did not hear and they did not incline their ear. They walked according to their own plans, in the stubbornness of their evil heart, and they went backwards and not forward.

---

[42]Reading *Qere* (hiphil perfect 1cs) instead of *Kethib* (hiphil perfect 3ms).

[25]From the day your fathers came out of the land of Egypt until today I sent you all my servants the prophets. I sent them persistently. [26]But they did not hear me; they did not incline their ear; they stiffened their neck; they did more evil than their fathers."

[27]"You tell them all these words but they will not listen to you. You will call to them, but they will not answer you.[43] [28]You tell them,
'This is the people which did not listen to the voice of YHWH its God and did not take instruction; Faithfulness has perished, it is cut off from their mouth.' "

Scholarly discussion of Jeremiah 7 often focuses on source and genre issues such as the scope of the so-called "Temple Sermon," the characteristics of such prose sermons, and their *Sitz im Leben*. The prevailing assessment recognizes the beginning of a new unit, addressed not to the people, but to the prophet, in v 16, limiting the Sermon, or some core, to vv 1-15.[44] Scholars usually divide into two groups on the issue of the origin and setting of the Temple Sermon. Some regard it as substantially authentic and consider it evidence for Jeremiah's critical stance toward

---

[43]Once again LXX preserves a shorter text consisting, substantially, of v 28 only ("You tell them this word, 'This is the people which did not listen . . . '"). Standard explanations as haplography (וְדִבַּרְתָּ אֲלֵיהֶם אֶת־כָּל־הַדְּבָרִים הָאֵלֶּה . . . וְאָמַרְתָּ אֲלֵיהֶם) or conflation (so J. Janzen, *Studies in the Text of Jeremiah*, HSM 6 [Cambridge MA: Harvard University Press, 1973] 37-38, 204n.8; cf. W. McKane, *Jeremiah*, 175-76) operate on classical text-critical assumptions. Alternatively, the material distinctive to MT (substantially v 27) may be analyzed in relation to MT's pattern of amplification of certain themes (e.g., the prophetic word as word of YHWH [see n. 17 above]), in this case, the "fruitlessness" of Jeremiah's mission.

[44]See, e.g., W. Thiel, *Redaktion*, 103-34, esp. 114, who reconstructs an original core prophetic saying consisting of vv 4, 9a, 10a*, 11*, 12(?), 14*; cf. T. Seidl, "Jeremias Tempelrede: Polemik gegen die joschijanische Reform? Die Paralleltraditionen Jer 7 und 26 auf ihre Effizienz für das Deuteronomismusproblem in Jeremia befragt," in *Jeremia und die "deuteronomistische Bewegung,"* ed. W. Gross, BBB 98 (Weinheim: Beltz Athenäum, 1995) 150-54.

the Josianic/Deuteronomic reform.[45] Others attribute substantially the entire unit (7:1–8:3) in its present form to the deuteronomistic editors of the book of Jeremiah and regularly focus on questions of the oral setting of such sermons.[46]

Assuming for the moment the deuteronomistic assessment of the style of the Temple Sermon and the role of deuteronomistic tradent-redactors in the formation of the book, the *Sitz im Buch* of Jer 7:1–8:3 deserves closer attention. In fact, in its final form, Jer 7:1-15 is not an independent "sermon." Rather, given the manner in which the narrative introduction/incipit controls Jer 7:1-28(8:3?), determining it all as one communication *to* Jeremiah, it does not report Jeremiah's sermon delivery, but Jeremiah's "reception" from YHWH of both the sermon to be delivered later (from the perspective of the final form of the book as reported in

---

[45]Those who consider the Temple Sermon authentic, antideuteronomic polemic include: A. Weiser, *Das Buch der Propheten Jeremia: Kapitel 1–25:13*, ATD 20 (Göttingen: Vandenhoeck & Ruprecht, ⁵1966) 60-69; J. Bright, *Jeremiah: Introduction, Translation, and Notes*, AB 21 (Garden City NY: Doubleday, 1965) 52-59; and W. Holladay, *Jeremiah*, 235-72. H. Weippert (*Prosareden*, 26-48) considers the prose sermons authentic, but sees them as evidence of Jeremiah's support of the deuteronomic program.

[46]Those who consider them the product of deuteronomistic redactors include: W. Rudolph, *Jeremia*, HAT 1/12 (Tübingen: J.C.B. Mohr, 1967³) 3; W. Thiel, *Redaktion*, 103-19; E. Nicholson, *Preaching to the Exiles*, 83-135; R. Carroll, *Chaos*, 21-24 and *Jeremiah*, 209-17; and W. McKane, *Jeremiah*, 164-66. For a recent survey of the current state of the question, see T. Seidl, "Jeremias Tempelrede," 141-47 (Seidl's own analysis leads him to conclude that the Temple Sermon is a "post-Jeremianic, exilic speech composition, which treats questions facing the exilic generation through the symbol of Jeremiah," 175). Nicholson argues that the prose sermons are evidence that deuteronomistically influenced tradent-redactors had a significant role in the formation of the final form of the book of Jeremiah. In Nicholson's view circles of deuteronomistic tradents and preachers adapted Jeremianic materials to their own situation in the exile. Their prose sermons on Jeremianic "texts" were later incorporated into the book of Jeremiah in passages such as Jeremiah 7:1–8:3. Among those who hold deuteronomistic interpretations, the question of the geographical setting of these deuteronomistic preachers (Babylon—pace Nicholson and others, or Judah—pace Carroll) comprises one of the more disputed issues in regard to prose sermons in the book.

Jeremiah 26[47]) and a private communication.[48] In contrast to composition techniques common in other portions of the book, Jer 7:1–8:3 avoids dialogue. Neither Jeremiah nor the people actually speak. Only YHWH's voice can be heard. YHWH tells Jeremiah what he will say, what the people have said, how the people will respond, and how Jeremiah will respond to them, in turn. Thus, Jer 7:1–8:3 may best be termed a "divine discourse." All figures other than YHWH (and the narrator) are only theoretically present; all voices are subordinate to YHWH's voice.

The control which the narrative introduction exerts breaks down to a degree in vv 20-21. Who says, "Therefore thus says the Lord YHWH/YHWH Sebaoth, the God of Israel"? Apparently YHWH refers to himself in the third person. The lack of clarity probably reflects the difficulties involved in maintaining the complex dialogue structure of this literary conceit. At any rate, vv 16-20 should probably be regarded as an aside to the prophet before YHWH resumes the communication of sermonic content in v 21.[49] The suggestion that vv 21-26 constitute an additional component of the (proposed) sermon finds support in the reassertion of the controlling literary conceit in vv 27-28. Here YHWH summarizes the instruction to Jeremiah to "tell them all these words."[50]

---

[47]Interestingly, Jeremiah 26 does not even imply the negative assessment of the likelihood that Judah will repent, avoiding entirely the prevalent tone of the private communication in Jeremiah 7.

[48]Obviously, the "private" aspect of this material applies only to the setting within the text. The text itself makes these private exchanges public. The distinction is significant, however, for a number of reasons. First, the notion that the "confessions" of Jeremiah represent the frustrations of a late period in the prophet's career depends upon the assumption that Jeremiah began his career optimistically. The book not only fails to support such an assumption, it actively resists it with the contention that YHWH privately revealed his full determination to punish from the outset. Second, discussions of the "authenticity" of the "confessions" often hinge on the private, intimate character of these texts. Jeremiah 7 illustrates, however, that deuteronomistic redactor-tradents were also capable of shaping materials as "private" communications.

[49]One notes the return of the 2mp address forms; the narrator-redactor-tradent shifts (prematurely, in anticipation of vv 27-28) to 3mp address forms in Jer 7:26.

[50]Similar difficulties arise with respect to 7:29–8:4. Jer 7:29 is an isolated

In the final form of the text, Jer 7:1-28 contains two broad categories of information, then: that meant for subsequent public delivery (vv 2b-15,21b-26) and that meant for Jeremiah's private consideration (vv 16-20, 27-28). How do the tone and content of these categories compare with one another? YHWH's private communication to Jeremiah stresses, first, the futility of any intercession on behalf of the people (7:16) and even of Jeremiah's preaching (7:27-28). It goes on, second, to detail reasons for this futility (idolatry, the people's unresponsiveness). Throughout, YHWH declares a firm intention to punish. The proposed sermon, on the other hand, seems to raise the possibility of repentance (7:3b-7). Significantly, however, YHWH ends the message very negatively ("And now because you did all these deeds . . . I will do to this house . . . just as I did to Shiloh. And I will cast you away . . . "). This unconditional statement concludes the message to be delivered publicly and conforms to the negative tone of the private communications. The somewhat paradoxical logic of the conditionals in the first half of the sermon, read in light of both the second half of the sermon and all the private communications, seems to be, "If you were to repent (but you will not) . . . and since you will not, I shall punish."[51]

Jeremiah 11:1-14

The second prohibition against intercession (Jer 11:14) occurs in a context very similar to the first (Jer 11:1-14). In addition to the prohibition, the so-called "Covenant Sermon" shares many features of the "divine discourse" structure demonstrated in Jer 7:1–8:3.

[1]The word which was to Jeremiah from YHWH, saying:

> [2]"Hear the words of this covenant and tell them to the people of Judah and the inhabitants of Jerusalem. [3]Tell them,

---

lament fragment including a second-feminine-singular reference to Jerusalem(?) Third-person references to the people couched in speech presumably addressed to Jeremiah resume immediately in Jer 7:30 and continue through Jer 8:3. Jer 8:4 constitutes an instruction for Jeremiah to speak the subsequent content publicly.

[51]T. Seidl ("Jeremias Tempelrede," 149) comments: "Throughout, the composition traverses a range of dimensions in a continuous elevation: from conditional promise to unconditional and final punishment."

Thus says YHWH, the God of Israel:

> "Cursed be the one who does not hear the words of this cove-
> nant [4]which I commanded your fathers on the day I brought
> them from the land of Egypt, from the furnace of iron, saying,
>> 'Hear my voice and do all that I command you and you
>> will be my people and I will be your God [5]so that I may
>> establish the promises which I promised your fathers: to
>> give them a land flowing with milk and honey (as it is to
>> this day).'

And I answered and said,
'So be it, YHWH'."

[6]And YHWH said to me,
> "Proclaim all these words in the cities of Judah and in the streets
> of Jerusalem, saying,
> 'Heed the words of this covenant and do them.' [7]For I solemnly
> admonished your fathers on the day I brought them from the land
> of Egypt, admonishing persistently, saying,
>> 'Heed my voice!'
> [8]But they did not heed and they did not incline their ear; Instead,
> they all walked in the stubbornness of their evil heart. And I
> brought on them all the words of this covenant which I commanded
> be done but they did not do [them]."

[9]And YHWH said to me,
> "Conspiracy is found among the men of Judah and the inhabitants
> of Jerusalem. [10]They have returned to the iniquities of their fore-
> fathers who refused to heed my words; they follow other gods to
> serve them; the house of Israel and the house of Judah have broken
> my covenant which I made with their fathers."

[11]Therefore thus says YHWH:
> "Behold, I am bringing evil upon them from which they will be
> unable to escape. They will cry out to me and I will not hear them.
> [12]Then the cities of Judah and the inhabitants of Jerusalem will go
> and cry out to the gods to whom they burn incense. But they will
> be totally unable to save them in the time of their distress.

[13]"For as many as your cities are your gods, Judah, and as many your streets, Jerusalem, are the altars you have set up to your shame, altars to burn incense to Baal.'
[14]So you (Jeremiah), do not pray for this people, and do not lift up a lament or a prayer for them, because I will not listen when they call to me in the time of their distress."

As in Jeremiah 7, YHWH's voice controls the Covenant Sermon although the structure of this discourse is not as complex. Following the unit introduced by the incipit (11:1-5a), four secondary level introductory formulas mark the contours of the discourse (11:5b, 6-8, 9-13, 14). Again, the redactor-tradent finds it difficult to maintain the literary conceit required by the third person reference to Jeremiah. Two of the three subsequent introductions refer to Jeremiah in the first person (11:6, 9). The prose narrator in the book of Jeremiah frequently alternates between formulas which refer to Jeremiah in the third person ("The word . . . which was to Jeremiah") and virtually identical formulas which refer to Jeremiah in the first person ("The word . . . which was to me"). Despite these first person formulas, which may be explained as attempts at verisimilitude, nothing of the prophet's personality or experience colors the material so introduced.

In fact, the dialogue structure of the Covenant Sermon serves the rhetorical purpose of directing the message of the Sermon to an audience unnamed in the text itself (the reader). The dialogue progresses in three movements. First, YHWH pronounces the gnomic curse on any who fail to obey the Covenant commanded to the Sinai generation. Jeremiah's "Amen" does not seem to be an expression of agreement to the charge to preach (v 2) but the expected liturgical response to the pronouncement of a covenant curse (compare Deut 27:15-26). Jeremiah affirms the principle which underlies YHWH's relationship with Israel.

Second, YHWH charges Jeremiah to proclaim in Judah and Jerusalem the history of disobedience to the Covenant and of YHWH's invocation of the curse. The oracle focuses, however, not on the audience but on "them" (that is, the ancestors) concluding with the confusing declaration that punishment has already visited Judah for the sins of the ancestors. LXX attests none of v 7 and only the last phrase of v 8 ("but they did not do [the words of this covenant]"). LXX avoids the confusing preoccupation with ancestral guilt, but it understands the final phrase of v 8 as a statement concerning Jeremiah's audience itself. It would then be an aside addressed to the reader. Either text represents alternative avenues to the same end. Both underscore the history of Judah's disobedience from a distance.[52]

At any rate, the distinction noted in the Temple Sermon between material meant for subsequent public delivery and material intended for the prophet's private consideration pertains in the Covenant Sermon, as well. The third and fourth subunits, vv 9-14, clearly address Jeremiah only. Notably, there is no charge to proclaim YHWH's decision to punish and all references to the people are in the third person. These subunits provide Jeremiah with information against which to understand the scope and purposes of his mission. He is to preach to a people whose fate has already been sealed. His efforts will be, in a sense, fruitless.

The sequence of data revealed to Jeremiah in this text is very important. YHWH informs Jeremiah that: the people have rebelled; they have returned to ancestral sin; they refuse to heed; they commit idolatry; they have broken the covenant. As a result—YHWH concludes definitively and irrevocably—they must be punished. They will cry, but YHWH will not hear. The prohibition against intercession culminates this sequence. Notably, according to the final form of the book, Jeremiah learns privately of YHWH's determination to punish at the same time he receives the commission to preach the Covenant Sermon. The prohibition, then, relates not to the failure or, better, forced termination of Jeremiah's intercessory efforts, but to the finality of YHWH's verdict.

In fact, the Sermon itself seems a purely hypothetical exercise. Jeremiah will exhort a people to obey YHWH. Yet, YHWH, knowing that they will not obey, has already reached a guilty verdict, a verdict which YHWH does not call upon Jeremiah to deliver. Furthermore, YHWH shares this information with the prophet from the outset. The Covenant Sermon

---

[52]See nn. 17 and 19 above for MT's emphasis on the divinely purposed sterility of Jeremiah's ministry. W. McKane (*Jeremiah*, 238-39), who does not note the relationship between MT's pluses in Jeremiah 7 and 11, comments poignantly concerning this particular instance: "the function of vv. 7-8 is to establish that from the time of the Exodus up to the present Yahweh, through his (prophetic) spokesmen, has unremittingly and urgently laid on his people the necessity of obedience to the terms of the covenant. Despite these solemn representations they have a record of unrelieved apostasy . . . vv. 7-8 . . . represent Yahweh's judgement as already complete. . . . "

portrays the prophet in the role of witness to the divine plan. The prophet understands YHWH's principles of relationship, he sees the history of failure, and, privately, learns the outcome planned for his own generation. He is not to "intercede" but "to stand before" YHWH in the divine council (compare Jer 23:16-22; 49:19-22 [50:44-46]; Amos 3:7; Isa 44:24-28; 46:9-11).

Who benefits from Jeremiah's testimony? Jeremiah's contemporaries are certainly not the beneficiaries. YHWH does not even commission Jeremiah to publish the verdict on Jeremiah's generation. Indeed, the verdict renders any other action on their behalf futile. As the narrator knows, the intended audience of Jeremiah's message are subsequent generations who can benefit from testimony to the certainty of YHWH's judgments according to the principles of the Covenant. The fate of Judah was no failure of divine protection, no accident of history.

Jeremiah 14:1–16:13

Unlike the setting of the other two prohibitions of intercession, the third prohibition in Jer 14:11-12 appears in the midst of largely unmarked poetic dialogue.[53] Laments and confessions of sin constitute components of the dialogue surrounding the prohibition. Indeed, the prohibition is but one unit in an extended compositional block concerned with the question of the efficacy of prayer genres and practices associated with seeking forgiveness and averting YHWH's anger.

14:1The word of YHWH which was[54] to Jeremiah concerning the "drought":[55]

---

[53]See above, 28-31.

[54]MT reads, literally, "which was the word of YHWH . . . " (אֲשֶׁר הָיָה דְבַר־יְהוָה). LXX has simply "And the word of YHWH was . . . " (καὶ ἐγένετο = וַיְהִי). While clearly MT is awkward, or more likely, corrupt, it is not untranslatable as it stands, especially in view of the frequency of narrative introductions of this type in the book of Jeremiah.

[55]בַּצָּרָה and the related form בַּצָּרוֹת, apparently derived from the verbal root בָּצַר, "to cut off, make inaccessible, enclose" (BDB, 130) occur only four times in the Hebrew Bible (Jer 14:1; 17:8; Psa 9:10; 10:1). The two instances in the Psalms refer generally to "trouble" (cf. RSV). The remaining instances in Jeremiah are usually translated "drought" (cf. LXX) on contextual grounds (references to drought conditions in Jer 14:2-6; "a tree planted by the water," Jer 17:8). Unfortunately, this translation, while appropriate, often prejudices

Speaker?—[2]"Judah mourns and her gates droop. . . . "

People—[7]"Although our sins witness against us, YHWH, act for your name's sake. . . . "

[10]Thus says YHWH to this people: "Indeed, they love to wander, they have not restrained their feet. . . . "

[11]And YHWH said to me:
"Do not pray for the well-being of this people. [12]Although they fast, I will not hear their cry; although they offer burnt offering and cereal offering, I will not be pleased with them; but with the sword, and by famine, and by pestilence I will consume them."

[13]And I said:
"Ah, Lord YHWH! Look! the prophets are telling them: 'You will not see sword and famine will not come to you; I will give you true peace in this place'."

[14]And YHWH said to me:
"[They are] false prophets prophesying in my name when I did not send them, I did not command them, and I did not speak to them. A false vision, worthless divination, and the deceits of their heart they prophesy to you."

[15]Therefore thus says YHWH:[56]

---

interpretations of Jer 14:1-22. Commentators usually set this passage against the context of some historical drought. Alternatively, the occurrence of the term at the extremes of the block of material concerning lament/confession/repentance, the clear metaphorical use in 17:8, and the paucity of material explicitly related to drought conditions (only Jer 14:2-6) suggest, rather, that the (unique) plural term in Jer 14:1 also refers to "troubles" in a broader sense.

[56]Normally, the introductory formula, "Therefore thus says YHWH," includes the עַל phrase which specifies the subject or the addressees of the subsequent oracle. In this instance, however, the "concerning" phrase involves a divine self-reference. MT's disjunctive punctuation suggests including the phrase in the quotation. While this rectifies the inconsistency, the situation probably reflects the editorial confusion attendant on the literary conceit that Jer 14:14 introduces vv 14-22 as divine speech.

"Concerning the prophets who prophesy in my name although I did not send them, who say that the sword and famine will not be in this land: By the sword and by famine these prophets will be consumed [16]and the people to whom they prophesy will be cast out in the streets of Jerusalem from famine and the sword and none will bury them—them, their wives, their sons, and their daughters—and I will pour out their evil upon them.

[17]And you tell them this word:
    'Let my eyes pour tears. . . . '"

[19]"Have you completely rejected Judah? . . . "

[15:1]YHWH said to me:
    "If Moses and Samuel stood before me, I would not be for this people;
    Send them from me and let them go! [2]And when they say to you,
        'Where shall we go?'
    You tell them,
        'Thus says YHWH:
            "Those for death, to death,
            those for the sword, to the sword,
            those for famine, to famine,
            and those for pestilence, to pestilence." '
[3]I will appoint over them four kinds (of destruction): the sword to kill, dogs to tear, birds of the air, and beasts of the field to consume and to destroy. [4]I will make them a horror to all the kingdoms of the earth because of what Manasseh, son of Hezekiah, king of Judah did in Jerusalem.

[5]Who will have compassion for you, Jerusalem? . . . "

[10]Woe to me, my mother, who bore me, a man of strife . . . to the whole land . . . they all curse me!

[11]YHWH said,
    "Have I not strengthened you for good? Have I not intervened for you with your enemies in time of evil and in time of trouble? [12]Can one break iron, iron from the north, or bronze? [13]Your wealth and your treasures I will give as spoil without charge for all your sins and in all your territories. [14]I will hand you over to your enemies in a land you do not know, for a fire is kindled in my anger; it burns against you."

[15]"You know, YHWH, remember me. . . . "

[19]Therefore, thus says YHWH,
"If you return, I will return to you and you will stand before me. . . . "

[16:1]And the word of YHWH was to me, saying:
[2]"Do not take a wife and have no children in this place!"

[3]For thus says YHWH concerning the sons and daughters born in this place and concerning their mothers who bear them and their fathers who beget them in this place:
[4]"They will die of deadly diseases; they will not be lamented; they will not be buried; they will be like dung on the ground; they will be exterminated by the sword and by famine; and their bodies will be food for the birds of the air and the beasts of the field."

[5]For thus says YHWH:
"Do not go to the house of mourning, do not go to lament, and do not mourn them for I have removed my peace from this people,"
—an utterance of YHWH—
"(my) steadfast love, and (my) mercy. [6]The great and the small in this land will die; they will not be buried; they will not be lamented; they will not be mourned; people will not shave their heads for them; [7]people will not break bread for the mourner[57] to console him for the dead; people will not give them the cup of consolation for his father or mother; [8]people will not enter the festal house to sit with them to eat and drink."

[9]For thus says YHWH Sebaoth, the God of Israel:
"Look! I will remove from this place, before your (plural) eyes and in your (plural) days, the sound of exultation, the sound of joy, the voice of the bridegroom, and the voice of the bride."

[10]"And when you (singular, Jeremiah) tell these people all these words and they say to you,

---

[57]Reading לָחֶם for לָהֶם with LXX, the Vulgate, and most commentators and versions; following Vulgate and most commentators regarding the repointing of אֵבֶל. See W. McKane, *Jeremiah*, 365.

'Why has YHWH spoken against us all this great evil? What are our iniquities and what are our sins which we have sinned against YHWH our God?'
[11]you tell them,
'Because your fathers abandoned me,'
—an utterance of YHWH—
'followed other gods, served them, worshipped them, abandoned me, and did not keep my Torah. [12]And you do greater evil than your fathers. Look! each one follows the stubbornness of his evil heart, not hearing me. [13]So I will hurl you form this land to the land which you do not known—you or your fathers—and there you will serve other gods day and night, for I will not show you favor'."

Exchanges[58] between YHWH and the prophet (14:11-16; 15:1-14; 16:1-13) seem to be related to one another ("sword, famine, pestilence" sequence) and are similar in tone, style, motif, and theology to the discourses in Jeremiah 7 and 11.[59] They punctuate the composition, dividing it into three sections: (1) a dialogue between YHWH(?) and the people (14:2-10) followed by the first exchange between YHWH and the prophet (14:11-16), (2) a second dialogue between YHWH and the people (14:17-22)[60] followed by the second (monologic) exchange between YHWH and the prophet, and (3) a third dialogue, now involving YHWH, Jerusalem, and Jeremiah, and including one of the so-called "confessions of Jeremiah" (15:5-21; "confession," 15:10-21) followed by the final divine discourse on the futility of ministry to this people.

In part because of the literary conceit fostered by the incipit (14:1), the identification of speakers in this composition is often difficult. Who

---

[58]Jeremiah 14:13, Jeremiah's objection that the false prophets have misled the people, represents the only exception to the monologue pattern characteristic of these prohibitions and their contexts.

[59]As in Jeremiah 7 and 11, the prohibitions in this composition have been customized to suit the context. In the Temple Sermon, YHWH's charges against the people concentrate on cultic crimes; in the Covenant Sermon, his charges center on covenant disobedience; in this lament composition which begins with a reference to drought conditions (14:1-6), YHWH threatens sword, famine, (14:12, 15-16; 15:2; 16:4) pestilence (14:12; 15:2; cf. 16:4), and captivity (15:2; cf. 16:13).

[60]See above, 36-38.

voices the descriptive lament over Judah in vv 2-6? What is the role of the prophet prior to v 13? How does one distinguish between the narrator, the prophet, and YHWH in vv 15-16? Of course, on one level this phenomenon points to the composition history of the section. Reconstruction of this history, however, presents its own problems, especially with regard to the question of "original" speakers and "original" settings.[61] On the canonical, level, however, the entire composition takes the form of a divine revelation. YHWH either cites or states the description of the situation (vv 2-6), cites the people's confession-petition (vv 7-9), and explains reasons for rejecting their petition. Significantly, YHWH addresses the entirety of this cited dialogue plus denial oracle to Jeremiah privately. As is the case with the Temple and Covenant Sermons, the narrative setting does not report Jeremiah's public delivery of this revelation. In fact, Jer 14:1–16:14 does not propose an eventual setting for the delivery of this material. When, if ever, were these words to be spoken publicly? What context is envisioned? Apparently, both the quoted dialogical exchanges and the divine discourses addressed to the prophet function exclusively as literary phenomena: through the services of the narrator-redactor, the reader has access to private information from the divine perspective. The text demonstrates little concern for the communication of YHWH's message to those immediately and directly concerned. For the most part, YHWH speaks entirely *to* Jeremiah *about* the people.[62] While the composition technique employed in Jer 14:1–16:13 (recontextualization of pre-

---

[61]Taken alone, vv 2-9 can be described as a communal lament in two parts: vv 2-6 are the statement of the situation prompting the lament and vv 7-9 are the confession of sin and petition for aid. Efforts to assign this lament to the prophet and deduce a prophetic intercessory ministry are purely speculative. They fail to account for the recontextualization effected by Jer 14:1 (a quotation of the people as revealed to Jeremiah by YHWH!) and 14:10 (YHWH's oracular response addressed to Jeremiah).

[62]The "private" nature of YHWH's discourse produces awkward effects, as, e.g., in Jer 16:1-14. Jer 16:5-7 shifts subtly (cf. W. McKane, *Jeremiah*, 366) from direct address to Jeremiah, to discussion of the condemned in the third person (but still addressed to Jeremiah), to language about the general principle specified in 16:5 (not only Jeremiah, but "no one" will lament them). Then, suddenly, v 9 introduces direct address to the people (2mp pronominal suffixes). "Private" communication resumes in v 10 and continues through v 13.

sumably preexisting materials) differs from that employed in Jer 7:1–8:3 and Jer 11:1-14 (apparently free composition), the rhetorical function conforms to that of the other prohibition contexts. In every case, the final form of the text purports to be divine discourse "privately" addressed to the prophet.

The literary conceit concerning voices in this passage finds a parallel in the problem of the situation assumed in it. The false prophets claim that there will be no crisis (14:13-15), but the incipit (14:1) and the people's lament (14:2-9) presuppose that a situation of crisis already exists. Beginning with YHWH's denial-oracle response to the lament and continuing throughout the complex, YHWH adopts the position that the *coming crisis* (the crisis which presumably already pertains?), will indeed come. Clearly, then, the complex represents a literary composition which functions solely on a literary level. From a retrospective vantage point, it juxtaposes voices and perspectives in such a way as to redefine claims and provide data unavailable to participants in the historical crisis. It is metadiscourse and metahistory.

In the Temple Sermon composition, YHWH's monologue explains that the sermon, itself, will be ineffective (as would any prophetic intercession) because the people have persistently refused to obey and will continue to do so. In the Covenant Sermon composition, YHWH's monologue reprises these themes, highlighting especially a long history of disobedience to the covenant. The "lament" composition turns attention to another aspect of the problem of YHWH's relationship with Judah. Is YHWH playing some game with the people issuing calls to repent yet rejecting confessions of sin (14:10)? What credibility does the public word of YHWH deserve if, behind the scenes, a private word of YHWH suggests that the people's fate is sealed ("because of what Manasseh, son of Hezekiah, king of Judah, did in Jerusalem," 15:4)?

The Prophet's Response

The book of Jeremiah preserves no evidence of a prophetic "intercessory" ministry, precisely understood. The phrase that appears with the greatest regularity in the context of the prophet's intermediation between the people and YHWH, עמד לפני, refers to the prophet's role as YHWH's representative, especially in matters of justice. Prior to Jer 19:14, the final form of the book demonstrates a programmatic interest in portraying YHWH's "private" revelation of his will to Jeremiah so that Jeremiah knows, from the outset, that YHWH's mind is set. Commentators often note the "private" or "personal" character of the "confessions." Presumably, in the final form of the text, the "confessions" represent Jeremiah's contribution to the "private" dialogue with YHWH. What, then, is the prophet's attitude toward YHWH's discourse?

The issue between Jeremiah and his opponents treated in the confessions, including YHWH's responses, involves the offence taken by the people at Jeremiah's preaching, not the failure of intercession as perceived by Jeremiah. Jeremiah's enemies seek to stop Jeremiah from preaching (11:21; 18:18; cf. 20:8,10). Jeremiah's complaints focus primarily on two points: (1) that he has only עמד לפני יהוה, that is, he has only delivered the message given him by YHWH (15:16; 17:16; 18:20; 20:8-11), and (2) that the delay in the fulfillment of YHWH's word, the delay of the punishment he announces, has made him vulnerable to attack (as a false prophet, 12:1-4; 17:15; 18:18; 20:10). YHWH's responses to the first three "confessions" call Jeremiah to fidelity to his assignment (11:21-22; 12:5; 15:19-21), in one case (11:21-22) employing language similar to the language of YHWH's private communications to the prophet in the Temple Sermon, the Covenant Sermon, and the Lament Composition. Jeremiah's "confessions," then, do not express sympathy with the people, nor do they disagree with YHWH's verdict on the guilty. Instead, they complain that YHWH is slow to judge and that the messenger is being blamed for the message. Contrary to the view that the arrangement of the book reflects a development in Jeremiah's view of the possibility of repentance, the "confessions" support the position of the "angry YHWH" voice in the book. Jeremiah's complaint against YHWH concerns the delay of punishment, focusing on YHWH's justice.[63] As Jeremiah knows, YHWH's verdict is final, repentance will be ineffectual, intercession is prohibited.

Characterization of the Voices in the Discussion

Three voices figure prominently in the discussion of YHWH's judgment on Judah. YHWH dominates. With very rare exceptions in the final form of the text, YHWH speaks virtually every word in his own voice or

---

[63]Cf. "stand before" theme and issues addressed, especially, in Jer 17:5-18; see chap. 4.

dictating speeches to the prophet or citing past or future statements by the people. Such is the focus on YHWH's voice that the text exhibits no interest in reporting even the bare fact of Jeremiah's public delivery of the prophetic message. The historical circumstances of Jeremiah's life and ministry do not concern the final form of the text of these divine discourses whatsoever. Jeremiah himself can only object to the pace of YHWH's plan and complain of the discomfort he experiences because of the harsh message he must preach. Of course, the narrator-redactor, who has gathered and shaped this material in this fashion, can be heard at points, but chiefly as a masking antivoice. The narrator-redactor is responsible for depicting the exchange between YHWH and Jeremiah as a private affair, a depiction which obscures what surely must have been an original public setting of at least some of this material. The narrator-redactor has little interest in the course of events during the career of Jeremiah, however. His/her interests lie with the universal workings of YHWH's mind.

Contours of the Discussion

Scholarship must take seriously the book's claim that the book of Jeremiah contains the words of YHWH. As mentioned above,[64] the current trend in scholarship is toward focusing on the persona of the prophet as the unifying key to the book of Jeremiah.[65] On several levels, however, the book, itself, claims to be the word of YHWH. (1) The tradition has explicitly identified several passages with complicated histories and now-mysterious origins (certainly some "historical" origin, in many, though not all, cases presumably in the career of the prophet) as the "words" of YHWH. (2) The so-called prose sermons have been cast as private revelatory events. They focus not on the public delivery of "sermons," but on the "private" reception of divine "discourses." Characteristically, these passages address the prophet directly and solely. Although private in character, however, these passages neither reveal nor demonstrate any significant interest in the inner thoughts of the prophet—neither the historical nor the literary figure. Instead, they concentrate on the delibera-

---

[64]See above, 4n.6, 15-17, 21-22, 28-38.

[65]See, e.g., M. Zulick, "The Agon of Jeremiah: On the Dialogic Invention of Prophetic Ethos," *The Quarterly Journal of Speech* 78 (1992): 125-48.

tions of YHWH. (3) Indeed, the entire book claims to be the word of YHWH revealed to Jeremiah (Jer 1:1, 2 LXX; Jer 1:2 MT).[66] This claim participates in the canonical shaping of the book. The focus shifts from the person of the prophet and the situation of his ministry toward YHWH's supraspecific perspective. The canonical book of Jeremiah is theological in the basic sense.

In this sense, the book of Jeremiah confronts the issue of theodicy. For example, whether in reference to the historical or the literary figure, scholars often emphasize Jeremiah's sympathetic identity with the people and/or with YHWH. In point of fact, at least in the texts examined above, Jeremiah is irrelevant except as he functions as a cipher for the exploration of theodicy. He is a voice. He stands over against people (and "before YHWH") as YHWH's spokesperson. Yet, he stands over against YHWH on the issue of justice. He complains to YHWH that YHWH does not bring punishment swiftly or severely enough. At the same time, he suggests that YHWH's judgment is insufficiently nuanced (that is, the righteous are punished along with the unrighteous).

The book of Jeremiah is theological in the basic sense because it embodies profound theological reflection concerning a series of polarities. The complexities of the discourse structure analyzed above allow for exploration of dimensions of YHWH's justice in relation to competing claims that YHWH offers sinners opportunities to repent and amend their behavior and that YHWH punishes surely and severely (Jeremiah 7). YHWH's grand scheme of history incorporates generation after generation in the Covenant principle of blessing and curse (Jeremiah 11). *Under normal circumstances* YHWH stands ready to hear and assist in times of trouble, but the circumstances of Jeremiah's generation are extremely abnormal. Despite the contention of false prophets that YHWH will preserve the status quo and despite the people's appeals to YHWH's promises and historical demonstrations on Israel's behalf, Judah's accumulated disobedi-

---

[66]The ancient versions of the superscription to the book attest to an editorial history for the superscription. While reconstruction of the details of that history is difficult and necessarily somewhat speculative, the final form of the superscription in the two major textual traditions (MT and LXX) demonstrates the traditions' interest in shifting attention to the book as the word of YHWH.

ence has reached proportions which demand YHWH's action. There are times when YHWH does not respond in mercy (Jer 14:1–15:4).

These issues resist simple solutions. The accommodation of mercy and justice as characteristics of a single deity—the problem of monotheism—cannot be reduced to precise formulas. The book of Jeremiah recognizes that a number of authentic perspectives *contribute* to a fuller understanding of YHWH's involvement in the history of his people.

"Liturgical" Materials in Jeremiah 7–20: The Worshipping Community and Its God in Dialogue[*]

Macroscopic examinations of the book of Jeremiah frequently explore certain prominent structural features such as the concentration of lament/confession materials in Jeremiah 7–20 or the similarly distributed prose sermons. In fact, as discussed above,[1] a common analytical approach to the macrostructure and composition history of Jeremiah sees these two blocks of material and their structural interrelationship as themselves key to the structure of Jeremiah 10–20.[2] While this approach has clearly identified a major "topographical feature" of the book of Jeremiah, one shortcoming of such solutions to the question of the structure and composition history of the book involves their failure to account for the structural and compositional role of so-called "miscellaneous" materials. From the perspective of polyphony and symphony, these analyses may prematurely privilege a given structuring voice or voices.[3]

---

[*]Portions of this chapter were read in the Formation of the Book of Jeremiah Consultation at the 1994 SBL Annual Meeting, Chicago, under the title "Liturgical Materials in Jeremiah 7–20: The Question of the Genre of a Prophetic Book."

[1]See 3-5, 15-17, 47-49.

[2]Note esp. M. Smith, *Laments*, 43-60.

[3]This shortcoming has been acknowledged by proponents of the prose sermon plus prophetic confession structural analysis. M. Smith, e.g., comments (*Laments*, 44):

> Against the background of this patterning of material, it is possible to clarify the arrangement of other materials contained in chapters 11–20. This formulation need not imply that this pattern had a redactional priority, i.e., that this pattern was an intermediate redactional stage in the development of chapters

Inquiries into the redaction history of Jeremiah, for example, tend to identify only the "deuteronomistic" redaction as a formative structure, typically refering to some texts as "postdeuteronomistic" but making little or no effort to discern structuring principles in these rather extensive "miscellaneous" materials.

One result of this fixation on the "deuteronomistic" book of Jeremiah is the potential failure to hear "voices" other than the admittedly predominant. Theoretically, at least, "postdeuteronomistic" and "miscellaneous" materials may be engaged in discussions reflecting other formative viewpoints.

As a test case, this chapter examines a category of materials in Jeremiah 7–20, namely a series of "liturgical" units, for want of a better name,[4] that seems to play a significant, if secondary, structuring role. These texts invite examination as a group for a number of stylistic, thematic, formal, and functional reasons. The entirety of Jeremiah 10, and especially 10:23-25 (a plea for YHWH's mercy citing a Psalm and a Proverb), Jer 12:14-17 (in language reminiscent of Jeremiah 10, YHWH promises mercy in the form of "instruction"), Jer 14:19-22 (another plea for mercy), Jer 16:21 (a judgment oracle promising "instruction"), Jer 17:5-13 (a wisdom composition concerning the consequences of "forsaking YHWH" and YHWH's capacity for distinguished judgment), and Jer 20:13 (a doxology praising YHWH for delivering the need from the hands of evildoers) advance a discussion of YHWH's justice on a plane quite distinct from the theodicy of the prose sermons or the complaints of the prophetic "confessions."

11–20. There is no way to verify such a suggestion; and there is no way of knowing what other units of material within chapters 11–20 were attached to one another, prior to the arrangement of introductory prose piece plus prophetic lament.

Smith goes on, however, to privilege the prose + confession structure as the *governing* structural feature of Jer 11–20. He agrees with K. O'Connor (*Confessions*, 111-12) that the "other" materials relate to this framing structure primarily through catchword connections and shared motifs and images.

[4]The "generic" literary character of these texts presents a major obstacle in attempts to locate them socially or historically.

[23]I know, YHWH,
> that one's ways are not *in one's control*;[5]
It is not for the one walking
> to direct one's steps.
[24]Reprove me,[6] YHWH, but in justice,
> not in your anger lest you diminish me.
[25]Pour out your wrath on the nations
> who do not know you
and on the families
> who do not call on your name.
For they have devoured Jacob,
> they have devoured him,[7]
>> they have consumed him,
>>> they have devastated his habitation.   (Jer 10:23-25)

[14]Thus says YHWH concerning all my evil neighbors who touch the inheritance which I[8] gave to my people Israel: Look! I will pluck them from their land and I will pluck the house of Judah from their midst. [15]And after I have plucked them, I will turn and have mercy on them and I will return each one to his inheritance and each to his land. [16]And if they will truly learn the ways of my people to swear by my name, "As YHWH lives!" just as they taught my people to swear by Baal, then they will be built in the midst of my people. [17]But if they will not listen, then I will surely pluck up that nation and and destroy—saying of YHWH.   (Jer 12:14-17)

[19]Have you completely rejected Judah?
> Is your soul disgusted with Zion?
Why are we smitten and there is no healing for us?
> We hope for peace and there is no good,
for a time of healing,

---

[5]MT reads לֹא לְאָדָם דַּרְכּוֹ, "not to a man his ways." Subsequent phrases suggest the notion of control over one's fate.

[6]LXX reads "us" here and in the next phrase.

[7]The second occurrence of the root אכל is not supported by a few manuscripts of LXX or by the parallel in Psa 79.

[8]Note the first-person reference. In this instance, the "thus says YHWH" indicates the omission of the intermediate step of transmission through a prophet. YHWH speaks for himself on the pages of the text.

and—look!—terror!
^{20}We know, YHWH, our wickedness,
     the guilt of our ancestors,
          for we have sinned against you.
^{21}Do not spurn for your name's sake!
     Do not abhor the throne of your glory!
Remember, do not break your covenant with us.

^{22}Are there among the nothings of the nations
          bringers of rain?
     Do the heavens give showers?
Is it not you, YHWH,
     our God—we hope in you—
who does all these things?   (Jer 14:19-22)

^{19}YHWH, my strength and my stronghold,
     my refuge in the day of trouble,
to you nations will come
     from the ends of the earth, and they will say:

"What falsehood we have inherited from our fathers,
     nothingness with no value in them.
^{20}Can a man make gods for himself?
     They are not gods!"

Therefore, look, I will make them know;
     in this instant, I will make them know
my hand and my might.
     And they will know that my name is YHWH.   (Jer 16:19-21)

^{5}Thus says YHWH:^{9}
     Cursed be the man who trusts in man,
          and makes flesh his arm
               and turns his heart from YHWH.
     ^{6}He will be like the shrub in the desert:
          He will not see good come.
     He will dwell in the parched places
          of the wilderness,

_____

^{9}LXX omits this phrase. See the discussion below, 138-40.

a land of salt without inhabitant.
[7]Blessed is the man who trusts in YHWH,
and YHWH is his trust.
[8]He will be like the tree planted by the waters:
He will send out his roots to the stream,
and he will not fear when the heat comes:
his leaves are green.
In the year of drought he will not be anxious,
and he will not cease bearing fruit.
[9]The heart is most deceitful and weak,
who can understand it?
[10]I, YHWH, examine the heart,
test the inward parts,
and give to each according to his ways,
according to the fruits of his deeds.
[11]A partridge hatching and it did not lay
(is like a man) making wealth but not justly:
In the middle of his days it will abandon him
and in the end of his (days) he will be a fool.

[12]O glorious throne,
exalted from the first,
place of our sanctuary!
[13]Hope of Israel, YHWH!
All who abandon you will be ashamed!

Those who abandon me will be written in the earth:
They have abandoned the fount of living water, YHWH.

(Jer 17:5-13)

[13]Sing to YHWH!
Praise YHWH!
For he has delivered the soul of the poor
from the hand of evildoers!   (Jer 20:13)

An Extended Dialogue

Several features of these texts suggest that they have been linked,
probably at a rather late stage in the redaction history of the book, as an
intertextual group. As a series of texts, they give the impression of a dialogue between YHWH and a representative or representatives of the people
on the subjects of YHWH's relations with Israel and the nations and

YHWH's ability to comprehend and appropriately requite human behavior. Three characteristics suggest an intertextuality among texts comprising this group.

Placement

The first feature linking these texts is placement. Following M. Smith's isolation of the material in 11–20 around the framework of prose + confession + YHWH's response proposed by W. Thiel and including Jeremiah 7–10,[10] analysis of the placement of these "liturgical" units reveals a significant pattern. In three cases these units appear prominently at or near the end of subdivisions (10:23-25; 12:14-17; 20:13). The remaining three units are extended compositions, appearing with equal prominence at the center of subdivisions: Jer 14:19-22 is part of the extended "prophetic liturgy" in Jeremiah 14, situated in the middle of the block Jeremiah 13-15; Jer 16:19-21 and 17:5-13 constitute an extended treatment of YHWH's role as judge of the individual human heart and are in turn situated between prose sections which frame the block Jeremiah 16-17. Four of these units very closely accompany prophetic confessions (12:14-17; 16:19-17:13*; 20:13).

Dialogical sequence

Read together, these units present a clear dialogical sequence. Polemic against idols, emphasizing the foolishness of human ways and the corollary notion of YHWH's status as sole God, dominates Jeremiah 10. The concluding confession that human beings cannot comprehend or govern their own paths forms a prelude to the request for mercy and the suggestion that YHWH punish the nations who have "devoured Jacob" and who call on other gods. In what seems almost a direct response to this petition, YHWH announces in Jer 12:14-17 the intention to spare those who have "touched the heritage" of the elect people if the transgressors will "learn the ways" of Israel and call on YHWH's name. Undaunted, a petitioner speaking in the plural later renews the plea for mercy in Jer 14:19-22 and appeals to YHWH's concern for his own reputation, acknowledging the ineptitude of the nations' idols. A few chapters later, in a strange rhetorical admixture (16:19-21), the petitioner moves from a doxology of YHWH as strength, stronghold, and refuge to a prediction

---

[10]See above, 12-13.

that the nations will come to YHWH and admit that their gods are worthless human constructions, no gods at all. YHWH, in turn, announces that he will "teach" them (lit. "make them to know") and they will know his name. This exchange opens into a treatment of the contrasting fates of those who trust in human strength and those who trust in YHWH. The justice inherent in these contrasting fates rests upon YHWH's ability to know the ineffable, namely the human heart, and "to give to all according to their ways, according to the fruit of their doings" (17:10). This discourse concludes with an ascription of praise to YHWH as the one who enforces this principle of justice, bringing shame upon all who forsake him (17:13). In the last of these "liturgical" units, the petitioner appeals to an audience to praise YHWH for delivering the poor (אֶבְיוֹן).

Common Vocabulary

A common vocabulary concerned with the themes of human folly, strict monotheism, and YHWH's relationship with the nations—themes elaborated in Jer 10:1-16—confirms suspicions of the literary interrelationship of these six texts. Knowledge—of the human heart, of the ways of nations, of YHWH—plays a central role in all these texts (ידע / למד, 10:23, 25; 16:21; 14:20; 17:9 [cf. 10:14] / 12:16 [cf. 10:2]). They refer conspicuously to the individual (אדם / גבר, 10:23; 16:20; 17:5 [cf. 10:14] / 17:5, 7) as well as the nations (גוי, 10:25; 12:17; 14:22; 16:19 [cf. 10:2, 7, 10]). The ways (דרך, 10:23; 12:16; 17:10 [cf. 10:2]) of both are inscrutable, at best, and downright folly, at worst. Only YHWH can comprehend the human heart (יסר, 10:24 [cf. 10:8]; בְּמִשְׁפָּט, 10:24; 17:11). The worthless gods of the nations (14:22; 16:19-20; 17:12-13? [cf. 10:1-16]) are no gods at all (הבל, 14:22; 16:19 [cf. 10:3, 8, 15]). The wise—of any nation—can place their trust and hope (קוה, 14:19, 22; 17:13; cf. כסא כבד, 14:21; 17:12) in YHWH. Indeed, the nations will one day realize the futility of their ways and the uselessness of their artificial gods and come to YHWH (12:14-17; 16:19). Nations who do not call on the name (שם ; cf. 10:6,16) of YHWH (10:25) and who have injured YHWH's people (אכל / נגע, 10:25 / 12:14) will one day learn the name (16:21): They will learn even to swear by that name (12:16) for whose sake YHWH shows mercy (14:21).

A Redactional Construction

The placement of these texts at strategic locations through Jeremiah 7–20 and the dual phenomena of evident interrelationship alongside a pluriform treatment of themes suggest that these texts owe their inclusion in the book of Jeremiah to a purely literary process. While a literary relationship between these texts seems clearly indicated, they do not comprise a uniform literary layer and relative priorities are difficult to ascertain. Certain indicators based on comparison of these texts to one another suggest (1) that their collocation in the book of Jeremiah or the establishment of literary links between them postdates the inclusion of the anti-idol polemic of Jeremiah 10, and (2) that they similarly comment on and extend the discussion of YHWH's justice broached in the "confessions" of Jeremiah.

First, Jer 10:23-25 fits rather smoothly in the context of the preceding lament (10:19-22) which belongs to the layer of materials concentrated in Jeremiah 8–9 and 14, typified by Jer 14:19-22. But Jer 10:23-25 subtly redirects the discussion from Jerusalem's immediate anguish to the more speculative issue of the mysterious ways of humanity and the appropriateness of YHWH's punishment, on the one hand, and to the comparatively greater guilt of the nations, on the other. The first of these two issues, then, governs Jer 17:5-13 and the second governs Jer 12:14-17 and 16:19-21. "Instruction" language, thematic in the anti-idol polemic of Jer 10:1-16, resurfaces centrally in 12:14-17 and 16:19-21; and the acknowledgement of YHWH's uniqueness, again a focal point of 10:1-16, assumes equal prominence in 12:14-17, 14:19-22, and 16:19-21.

Second, Jer 10:23-24 and 17:5-13 draw attention to dimensions of YHWH's justice not addressed in the *Gerichtsdoxologien* of the prose sermons and only implied in the "confessions," namely the question of the propriety and justice of YHWH's punishment on the individual level. The prose sermons frequently refer to YHWH's acts as responses to the "ways and deeds" of the people. But, as Jer 10:23-24 and 17:5-13 point out, human "ways and deeds" are both mysterious and, above all, *individual*. They intensify the implication of the "confessions" that YHWH's reputation for justice must also be measured against the experience of the righteous individual amidst sinners (see Jer 20:13).

In the end, these texts seem to function as a matrix interconnecting several otherwise independent Jeremianic themes in a subtle discussion of YHWH's character and will: How do monotheism, Israel's place among the nations, and YHWH's reputation for justice even at the individual level interrelate? Nevertheless, several phenomena suggest that this interrelationship resulted from a complicated process of growth.

Semantic Variation

Passages exploit different aspects of the semantic range of key terms common to many or all of these texts. For example, the rich term דֶּרֶךְ "way" refers to (1) the course of a human life, the fate of an individual (10:23; compare צַעַד and Job 14:16; 31:4); (2) the mysteries of human existence which only YHWH can know (10:23; 17:10); and (3) a given nation's religio-ethical customs—both Israel's customs to be emulated (12:16) and the nations' to be avoided (12:16; see 10:2). The first usage refers to the very private inner life of individuals and the third to the very public life of communities. Similarly, the phrase כִּסֵּא כָבוֹד, "glorious throne," either refers to Mt. Zion as the seat of the cult (14:21) or functions as a circumlocution for YHWH himself (17:12).

Conceptual Variation

Tensions also become apparent on a conceptual level. The opening passage in the series (10:24) calls upon YHWH to judge not according to deserts (בְּמִשְׁפָּט) but in mercy. Another (17:9-13) expresses confidence in the fact that YHWH cannot be misled by appearances, but will search the hidden realm of the human heart. YHWH can be trusted, then, to judge according to deeds and fruits. Similarly, the opening passage calls upon YHWH to punish those who have "consumed" (אכל, 10:25) Jacob; but a subsequent passage (12:15) announces YHWH's intention to have mercy on those who have "touched" (נגע) his heritage. Indeed, the speaker in 16:19-21—on a synchronic level, presumably the same speaker who pled for punishment on the nations in 10:23-25—predicts the day when the nations will voluntarily come to YHWH.

Three other characteristics provide additional support for this conclusion: evidence of intertextual relationships on a canonical level; generic features consistent with *Schreibtischarbeit*; and an extreme ambiguity, even confusion, with respect to the identity of speakers.

Canonical Intertextuality

Individual texts in the series allude to and even cite texts in Jeremiah and in a wide range of other books, perhaps suggesting growth of a canonical awareness. For example, the widely recognized composite nature of Jer 10:23-25 which cites Prov 16:9[11] and Ps 79:6-7 seems almost an announcement of an intention to relate the message of the book of Jeremiah to the literatures of the cultic community and of reflective wisdom theology. The plea to YHWH that he guard against wrathfully and unjustly "diminishing" his people alludes to the influential Leviticus 26 (מעט in the sense of "to diminish/decimate a people" occurs only in Jer 10:24; Lev 26:22; and Ezek 29:16 [of Egypt]).

Jer 12:14-17, on the other hand, appropriates the familiar "building" and "destroying" language of Jeremiah's call, but reshapes it to new purposes. "To pluck up" occurs four times in this passage and assumes multiple meanings.[12] A dual use of the term describes the manner in which YHWH will "pluck up" both his enemies and his people in one act. The first use, in the general sense of "to punish," is not unusual *prima facie*; but the second, in the sense of "to save," is unique.[13] The third occurrence conforms to the first usage. The fourth and final use of the term, however, while reflecting the usual destructive sense, presents an intriguing set of difficulties. Does it refer to an action subsequent to YHWH's compassionate return of the nations to their homelands? Or does it explicate the original uprooting in terms of the choices YHWH faces, namely, either a "partial" uprooting in the case of a nation willing to convert or a total annihilation in the other case? Neither possibility portrays a smooth sequence of events. Indeed, such difficulties have led many to view 12:14-17 as a composite of vv 14-15, a postexilic comment inspired by the theme of "heritage" in the preceding passage, and vv 16-17 as an even later comment on vv 14-15 interested in mitigating their

---

[11]G. von Rad, e.g., found the dependence of Jer 10:23 on Prov 16:9 undeniable (*Wisdom in Israel* [Nashville: Abindgon, 1972] 100n.2).

[12]LXX resorts to three distinct verbs (ἀποσπάω "to tear away," ἐκβάλλω "to cast out," and ἐξαίρω "to lift away") to translate נתש. LXX also uses the second verb to translate both the second occurrence of the idea in v 14 and the first occurrence in v 15, thereby confusing the issue of whether YHWH's promise of restoration in v 15 applies to Israel or to the nations.

[13]See P. Volz, *Der Prophet Jeremia*, KAT 10 (Leipzig: A. Deichertsche Verlagsbuchhandlung, 1920) 112.

apparent universalism by providing a condition for YHWH's mercy.[14] At any rate, Jeremiah 12:14-17 seems to be a late composition drawing upon many elements of the existing Jeremiah tradition to build a picture of a day when the nations may choose the true God as their own.

The vocabulary of Jer 14:19-22 bears significant affinities with a wide spectrum of very late texts. The aggregation of terms for sin (פשע, עון, and חטא) characterizes postexilic texts such as 1 Kgs 8:47 = 2 Chron 6:37; Psa 106:6; Dan 9:5,15; and Neh 9:33.[15] The clearest parallel use of מאס is Lam 5:22 (cf. also Psa 78:59,67). Apart from this passage, only Deut 32:19 and Lam 2:6 employ נאץ of YHWH. The polemic against idols in v 22 (הבל) stands in the tradition of very late texts in the book of Jeremiah (2:5; 8:19; 10:3,15 = 51:18; 16:19),[16] late-redaction Deuteronomistic texts (Deut 32:21; 1 Kgs 16:13,26; 2 Kgs 17:15), and Trito-Isaiah (Isa 57:13). Clearest parallels to the expression of confidence, "we hope in you," occur in late sections of Jeremiah (14:8,22; 17:13; 50:7) and Isaiah (25:9; 26:8; 33:2). In addition to these general similarities in tone and vocabulary between Jer 14:19-22 and widely dispersed late exilic and postexilic texts, a more direct intertextual relationship seems to exist with a specific key postexilic text. In fact, although such dependencies are difficult to establish, Jer 14:19-22 reads like a prayer composed in response to the prescription in Lev 26:40-45: ". . . if they confess their iniquity

---

[14]Scholars propose various analyses of Jer 12:14-17, most of which agree that, at least in its final form, the unit postdates Jeremiah. The chief points of debate concern whether vv 14-17 includes some Jeremianic core (so W. Rudolph and C. Cornill [*Das Buch Jeremia* (Leipzig: Chr. Herm. Tauchnitz, 1905)]) and whether the non-Jeremianic component dates to the exilic (so W. Thiel, *Redaktion*, 162-68, who attributes the entire unit to D) or the postexilic periods (vv 14-17: B. Duhm and P. Volz; vv 15-17: W. Rudolph). W. McKane (*Jeremiah*, 283-84) argues that the entire unit is a "'composition' in the sense that it is composed from preexisting passages of scripture, especially the definition of Jeremiah's prophetic office in the call narrative . . . and the notices about the exile and restoration of Judah's neighbours in the foreign oracles of the book of Jeremiah." In his view, 12:7-11; 48:47; and 49:6 ("I will restore the fortunes of [one of Israel's neighbors]") generated vv 14-15; vv 16-17 offer an alternative exegesis of YHWH's promise to restore Israel's neighbors.

[15]Cf. Bak, *Klagender Gott*, 59 (esp. n. 116) and 61-64.

[16]Cf. Biddle, *Redaction*, 148-54.

and the iniquity of their ancestors . . . then I will remember my covenant with Jacob . . . I will not spurn them, or abhor them so as to destroy them utterly and break my covenant with them, for I am the LORD their God. . . ." In Jer 14:19-22 the people do indeed confess their own and their ancestors' iniquity, and they call upon YHWH not to spurn or abhor them (מאס and גּעל coincide only in Jer 14:19 and Lev 26:15,43, 44) but to remember and not to break the covenant.[17] They remind YHWH of his relationship to them (Jer 14:22; Lev 26:45).

Observations regarding the late milieu of the polemic against idols in 14:19-22 apply to Jer 16:19-21, as well. As McKane comments, "Such Jeremianic vocabulary as can be detected in vv 19-21 has been transported to a new setting: שֶׁקֶר, הֶבֶל, and אֱלֹהִים וְהֵמָּה לֹא אֱלֹהִים are not being used of Israel's insensate idolatry but of the idolatrous Gentile world."[18] Additionally, v 19a most closely parallels affirmations of confidence in the Psalms (37:39; 46:2; 59:17; 61:4; cf. Nah 1:7).

The psalmic style of Jer 17:5-13 and 20:13 is unmistakable and long-noted. While no clear one-to-one correspondences between these texts and texts outside the book of Jeremiah can be established,[19] it is difficult

---

[17]The possibility of YHWH "breaking the covenant," פָּרַר בְּרִית comes under discussion rarely, most notably once again in Jer 14:21 and Lev 26:44. Cf. also Judg 2:1 and Jer 33:20-21, part of the longest passage in the book of Jeremiah not represented in LXX, and thus probably later than Jer 14 (see M. Biddle, "The Literary Frame Surrounding Jeremiah 30:1–33:26," *ZAW* 100 [1988]: 409-13; P.-M. Bogaert, "Urtext, texte court et relecture: Jérémie XXXIII 14-26 TM et se préparations," *SVT* 43 [1991]: 236-47; and, Y. Goldman, *Prophétie et royauté au retour de l'exil: Les origines littéraires de la forme massorétique du livre de Jérémie*, OBO 118 [Göttingen: Vandenhoeck & Ruprecht, 1992] 9-56).

Jer 33:20-21 promises precisely what the people seek in 14:21. The question of the permanence and reliability of YHWH's covenant apparently sparked another intertextual discussion in the book of Jeremiah. The redactional observation that texts such as 14:21 can be appropriated by multiple intertextual discussions strengthens the argument that the book of Jeremiah must be read as a complex matrix of intertextual dialogue and comment.

[18]*Jeremiah*, 382.

[19]Commentators commonly note striking similarities between Jer 17:7-8 and Psalm 1, although the question of dependency cannot be settled. R. Carroll (*Jere-*

to deny the scholastic tone of the former passage or the liturgical nature of the latter. Neither bears the expected marks of prophetic speech. Parallels to the wisdom genres of malediction and macarism are exceedingly numerous (Psalms 1; 31; 34; 118; etc.) and the call to communal praise is a common element in both songs of thanksgiving and laments (Ps 22:21; 33:19; 56:14; 120:2; etc.; cf. Isa 42:10; 1 Chron 16:9,23).

Generic Incongruities

In addition to indicators of intertextual relationships between these passages and later texts outside the book of Jeremiah, two remarkable instances of generic incongruity also point to the redactional nature of the texts in question. Jer 16:19-21 consists of three distinct subunits in a remarkable combination. The initial first-person-singular ascription of praise celebrates YHWH as the speaker's source of strength and refuge. Such exclamations normally appear in songs of thanksgiving or petitions for deliverance. This ascription of praise, however, introduces a prediction, addressed to YHWH, concerning the future conversion of the gentiles. Nowhere else in the Hebrew Bible does an individual—prophet or otherwise—*inform YHWH* of the course which human history will take, *in particular not with respect to YHWH's relationship with the nations.* In addition to the unusual level of audacity and the unique combination of elements, the internal logic of the sequence seems, at best, obscure. How does the declaration of confidence suggest that the nations will abandon their idols and come from the ends of the earth to YHWH? The unit concludes with an oracle (of judgment?) introduced by לָכֵן. Again the argument progresses according to an eccentric logic. In response to the prediction that the nations will recognize the error of idolatry, YHWH de-

---

miah, 351), e.g., concludes that the differences in tone exclude the possibility of dependency in either direction. J. Thompson (*Jeremiah*, 421) argues that since both Jer 17:7-8 and 12:1-2 refer to Psalm 1 Jeremiah may had access to it. At any rate, both Carroll and W. McKane (*Jeremiah*, 391-92) insightfully point to a significant distinction with respect to the individual focus of Jer 17:5-8 in comparison to Psalm 1 and other texts (Isa 31:3 and Jer 2:37) adduced as parallels. These parallel passages concern trust in institutional structures (Torah piety in Psalm 1; political alliances in Isaiah 31 and Jeremiah 2) in the context of corporate life. Jer 17:5-8, on the other hand, discusses the individual's private trust in YHWH.

clares the intention to teach a violent lesson. This strange sequence has led many to see v 21 as the original continuation of v 18.[20] At any rate, based upon the generic features of this unit, one can reasonably conclude that it was "cobbled together" in an artificial and rather haphazard manner.

The discordant shift of tone and discourse at Jer 20:13 has long presented exegetes with a formal puzzle. Is this call for communal praise a predictable component in an individual lament and thus a continuation of 20:7-12,[21] or do its plural verb forms and third-person references to the אֶבְיוֹן mark it as an editorial insertion, perhaps even "the praise song of the community" which "bears the word."[22] The use of אֶבְיוֹן in a manner otherwise known only in late postexilic ideological piety and the position of 20:13 in analogy to the other "liturgical" texts under consideration tilt the scales in favor of redactional origins. Thus the jarring effect of the unit, from a generic viewpoint, finds a redaction-critical explanation.

Ambiguous Speakers

A final phenomenon that apparently indicates the redactional nature of several of these units (10:23-25; 16:19-21; 17:12-13) is confusion of the identity of speakers. MT and LXX disagree as to the speaker(s) in 10:23-25 and neither rendition sits comfortably in the context. MT begins with an ambiguous first-person singular which continues through v 24 before shifting to a third-person reference to Jacob. LXX begins with second-person singular address directed to YHWH, shifts in v 24 to first-person plural, and concludes as does MT. The nearest possible antecedent for MT's first person is the personified Jerusalem of 14:19-21,[23] although the phenomenon of Mother Jerusalem commenting on the vagaries of

---

[20]See W. McKane, *Jeremiah*, 380-83. Even J. Thompson, who generally assumes authenticity, admits that the structure of vv 19-21 defies easy explanation (*Jeremiah*, 414): "[They have] been grouped with other material in ch. 16 for a reason best understood by the editor."

[21]So, among others, M. Smith, *Laments*, 27; K. O'Connor, *Confessions*, 69.

[22]V. Herntrich, *Jeremia: Der Prophet und sein Volk: Eine Einführung in die Botschaft des Jeremia* (Gütersloh, 1938) 17 (cited in Bak, 205); see also B. Duhm, *Jeremia* (cited in W. Holladay, *Jeremiah*, 549); W. McKane, *Jeremiah*, 481-82.

[23]See above, 20-21.

human nature or referring to Jacob in the third person has no obvious parallel. LXX seems to reflect a sensitivity to these peculiarities, although a putative antecedent for its first-person-plural pronouns is even more difficult to identify.[24]

Only YHWH speaks in Jeremiah 16:1-18. As a result, the source of the sudden exclamation, "My strength and my refuge!" in 16:19 can only be surmised. Perhaps the prophet, addressed directly in 16:10, proclaims confidence in YHWH. But the unusual nature of the remainder of the statement points in another direction: the sudden appearance of a human voice can best be attributed to editorial and theological concerns. This passage voices a fatalism otherwise virtually unknown in the book of Jeremiah and very rare, indeed, in the prophetic literature. It stops only just short of charging YHWH with injustice, implying that YHWH indulges his anger beyond appropriate measure. According to this voice, YHWH not only vindictively overpunishes, he misdirects his indignation against relatively innocent Judah instead of her criminal neighbors.

Finally, the communal (first-person-plural) doxology in Jer 17:12-13 appears equally abrupt, ambiguous, and unanticipated. Uncertainty concerning the contextual identity of the speakers notwithstanding, the psalmic tone of this passage recalls other such texts which deal with the deliverance of righteous individuals, namely Jer 10:23-25; 17:5-13. Does Jer 20:13 celebrate the resolution of the problem raised in these texts?

Subtle Theological Reflection

To this point the argument has focused on establishing (1) that these texts are redactional, i.e., that they have either been composed or appropriated rather mechanically as part of a rather unmistakable editorial effort (or, given the degree of tension which exists between them, probably a combination of these two methods) and (2) that they belong together, that is, in the current form of the text they participate in a single, though "artificial," discussion. It remains to analyze the argument of this redactional "voice."

---

[24]W. McKane (*Jeremiah*, 233) cites Jerome's comment, "According to the Hebrew, Jerusalem herself speaks . . . according to LXX it is the prophet." McKane chooses to regard MT's first person as evidence of the prophet's amorphous identification with his community.

Two themes dominate these "liturgical" texts: (1) YHWH, the nations, and their gods, and (2) wisdom speculation concerning YHWH and the individual's heart. At issue with respect to the first theme is the question of how YHWH will deal with the nations, idol-worshipers and enemies of Israel. Will he punish those who have harmed Jacob? (He will, but only within limits.) Afterward he will extend the opportunity to "learn the ways" of his elect, i.e., to convert to the worship of YHWH, and thus to enjoy his blessing. Indeed, since the idols of the nations are no-gods-at-all, deceptions unable even to bring rain, the nations will one day awaken to a new awareness of the reality that only YHWH is God, only YHWH acts. In that day they will come to worship YHWH. At issue with respect to the second, intriguingly related, theme associated with wisdom speculation is the question of YHWH's ability discriminately to judge human behavior. Human beings cannot direct/comprehend their own paths. YHWH, who alone understands, must have mercy. Unless he spares for the sake of his name, of his "glorious throne," of his promise, Israel has no hope. In the end, YHWH can be trusted not only to bring justice on the macroscopic level of entire nations, using the blunt instrument of human armies, but to weigh individual hearts. His criterion will not be membership in a community, but the purity of the individual's heart, mind, and ways.

Investigation of the structure and composition of Jer 16:19–17:18 indicates that these two themes constituted major concerns at some stage in the growth of the book. Research on the "confessions" has shown that the LXX, or the first edition of Jeremiah as it has come to be called, regarded them less in terms of the specifically personal Jeremiah and more in terms of the universal. That is, the LXX portrays the suffering of a righteous individual, perhaps as a representative of the community or even better as a representative of Everyperson, rather than the suffering of the particular individual Jeremiah.[25] The "liturgical" materials explore related themes. They examine YHWH's relationship to individuals, regardless of ethnicity, in terms of the general principles which characterize

---

[25]See A. Diamond, "Jeremiah's Confessions in the LXX and MT." Interestingly, MT seems to manifest conflicting trends. Diamond has identified MT's accentuation, in comparison to LXX, of the prophet as an individual in the "confessions." MT also accentuates, in comparison to LXX, the status of the written word as the word of YHWH in a manner which turns attention away from the prophet.

YHWH's ability to discern motivations and true character. Significantly, these two bodies of material converge in Jer 16:19–17:18 in such a way as to confirm the conclusions of confessions research and to suggest that an interest in universally applicable theological insights characterized a major stage in the redaction history of the book of Jeremiah.

An Analysis of Jer 16:19–17:18*

A framework of mostly deuteronomistic prose[26] dealing with Judah's failures and punishment surrounds the extended metrical composition Jer 16:19–17:18. In contrast, Jer 16:19–17:18, itself, except for 17:1-14, deals rather with the nations, Everyperson, YHWH's ability to discern inner motivations, and the prophet as the representative of the universal condition.

Interestingly, Jer 17:1-4, which echoes the prose theme of Judah's sin in language at least heavily influenced by the deuteronomistic tradition in the book of Jeremiah, constitutes a doublet in MT represented only once in LXX (Jer 15:13-14). This phenomenon has long excited the interest of students of the problem of the relationship between MT and the significantly shorter and "reordered" LXX.[27] Recognizing that this larger problem lies well beyond the scope of this chapter and that, in the example at issue, the evidence is ambiguous (for example, 15:13-14 does not sit well in its context, since it addresses the people in response to the prophet's

---

[26]The deuteronomistic character of this prose is indicated by phraseology such as the formulaic description of the catastrophe awaiting the people (16:4, 6, 9), the question-response concerning the reason for judgment (16:10-13), and the stereotypical deuteronomistic charges that the people have "forsaken me . . . and gone after other gods . . . " (16:11-12) and have "not listen[ed] or incline[d] their ear; they stiffened their necks and would not hear or receive instruction" (17:23, 24, 27). Jer 16:14-15 constitutes the single clear exception. Unlike the other prose in Jeremiah 16-17, it promises a return of the people to the land in a second Exodus to transpire *after* the crisis predicted (*ex post facto*). In addition to the distinctively late subject matter, it also begins with the "eschatological" formula which characteristically introduces several other very late redactional units in the book and includes the "it shall no longer be said X but Y" scheme also common to this material. See M. Biddle, "Literary Frame," 410.

[27]See F. Hubmann, *Konfessionen*, 219, and the recent study devoted to the question of doublets in evaluating MT and LXX by Y. Goldman (*Prophété et royauté*), among others.

personal[?] complaint),[28] several factors mitigate confidence in the majority position of interpreters who favor MT.[29]

First, as noted, Jer 17:1-4 disrupts the flow of the discussion in the Everyperson composition. Second, Jer 17:1-4 resembles a composition based on fragments of Jeremianic tradition. The reference to "beside every green tree, and on the high hills, on the mountains in the open country" employs a derivative of the common "on the high hills and under every green tree" (Jer 2:20).[30] Third, only v 1 contains new material. But it seems designed to establish the link between 17:1-4 and its context (for "written" and "heart," see 17:9, 13, respectively, for "sin of Judah" theme and "heritage," see 16:1-18). These usages do not constitute precise parallels, however. Jer 17:1 describes Judah's sin, inscribed on their hearts, in a manner which suggests unforgivable corporate guilt; Jer 17:9-13 discusses the dynamics of individual responsibility and individual choice. Fourth, MT's nonsensical "Thus says the Lord" (17:5) introduces a unit which neither purports to be nor functions as YHWH speech. At least with respect to this phrase, LXX's zero variant seems preferable.[31]

---

[28]For a discussion of the exilic treatment of the theme of the suffering of the innocent righteous in the "confessions" of Jeremiah, see, most recently, D. Bak, *Klagender Gott*, esp. 220-31. See also E. Gerstenberger, "Jeremiah's Complaints;" A. H. J. Gunneweg, "Konfession oder Interpretation;" D. Clines and D. Gunn, "Form, Occasion and Redaction in Jeremiah 20," *ZAW* 988 (1976): 390-403.

[29]So, e.g., W. Rudolph, *Jeremia*, 97 (homoioteleuton); J. Thompson, *Jeremiah*, 416n.1 ("lacking in LXX for a reason that is not now clear"); W. McKane, *Jeremiah*, 384; R. Carroll (*Jeremiah*, 349) regards v 2 as a later expansion.

[30]Cf. W. Holladay, "'On Every High Hill and Under Every Green Tree'," *VT* 11 (1961): 170-76.

[31]MT's tendency to designate units of various sizes and at various levels as YHWH-speech, observable also to a lesser degree in LXX, has already been noted. As MT stands, YHWH-speech begins in 16:21 and continues in two sections (17:1-4, 5-10[11?]) until the "liturgical" response in 17:12-13. In the resultant composition, YHWH announces his intention to one day reveal his power, might, and name to the nations; following a condemnation of Judah's sin-hardened hearts, he then elucidates the wisdom/deuteronomistic principle of blessing/cursing. He concludes with an assurance that he judges the secrets of the heart, requiting individuals according to the true assessment of their ways and deeds. Thus, MT does not avoid the (theo)logical difficulties which arise in the LXX version of this com-

At any rate, the LXX text of 16:19–17:18, omitting 17:1-4, exhibits a remarkable degree of structural, albeit apparently editorial, cohesion. Exegetes who read 16:21–17:4 as a logical continuation of 16:16-18 usually regard 16:19-21 as disruptive. Normally, these commentators interpret 17:(1-4)5-18 as a series of more-or-less discrete units.[32] Alternatively, 16:19-21 may function as an integral element in the extended composition, 16:19–17:18. Jer 17:1-4 may be the secondary or even intrusive element representing the editorial effort to link more firmly the universal theme of 16:19–17:18 with the specifics of the prose discussion of Judah's sins.

Indeed, several structural features suggest that Jer 16:19–17:18* may constitute an extended editorial composition. The phrase "day of trouble/ evil" (בְּיוֹם צָרָה, 16:19; בְּיוֹם רָעָה, 17:17; יוֹם רָעָה, 17:18; cf. וּבִשְׁנַת בַּצֹּרֶת, 17:8) forms an inclusio demarcating the extended composition. Jer 17:5-18 may be arranged in three sections almost equal in length (8,8, and 7 lines each) mirroring the distinct tripartite structure of 16:19-21 in an ABC//B'C'A' arrangement. The first two lines of the introduction (Jer 16:19a,b) invoke YHWH as source of strength and salvation and go on to discuss the deliberations of the (enemy-)nations; the parallel stanza (17:14-18) invokes YHWH as healer, savior, and praise and continues with a discussion of the enemies' deliberations. The middle section of the introduction (16:19c-20) reports the nations' confession of the futility of their trust in gods of human manufacture (הֲיַעֲשֶׂה־לּוֹ אָדָם אֱלֹהִים); the corresponding stanza (17:5-8) contrasts the fates of those who trust in human strength (יִבְטַח בָּאָדָם) and those who trust in YHWH (יִבְטַח בַּיהוָה). The nations' gods are useless; similarly, those who trust in "man" are fruitless. Those who trust in YHWH bear fruit without ceasing. In the final section of the introduction YHWH declares his

---

position. Instead, YHWH's assertions, themselves, raise the issue of his justice. Retroverting the argument, both MT and LXX claim that YHWH unfailingly responds with reward or punishment according to the character of the individual. No less than does Job, Jeremiah directly confronts this issue, however. The logic of this argument would dictate the guilt of all of those who suffered during the Babylonian crisis (cf. Jer 5:1-5). The "confessions" object that Jeremiah, at least, was guiltless. Yet he suffered at the hands of his "enemies."

[32]The positions of the commentators are conveniently summarized in W. McKane, *Jeremiah*, 380-83.

intention to make his might and reputation known instantaneously (16:21); the middle section of the body of the composition focuses on YHWH's status as Israel's hope and source of life and his ability to know.

Structure of 16:19–17:18*

Inclusio—"day of trouble/evil" (בְּיוֹם צָרָה)   *16:19*

A—Yahweh as source of strength and salvation:
        the deliberations of the (enemy-)nations   16:19a,b
    B—the nations' futile trust in gods
        of human manufacture (הֲיַעֲשֶׂה־לּוֹ אָדָם אֱלֹהִים)   16:19c-20
        C—YHWH intends to make his might and
            reputation known instantaneously   16:21

. . . .

    B'—trust in human strength (יִבְטַח בָּאָדָם)
        contrasted with trust in Yahweh (יִבְטַח בַּיהוָה)   17:5-8

"year of trouble/evil" (וּבִשְׁנַת בַּצֹּרֶת)   *17:8*

        C'—God as Israel's hope and source of life
            and his ability to know   17:9-13
A'—Yahweh as healer, savior, and praise;
        the enemies' deliberations   17:14-18

Inclusio—"day of trouble/evil"   (בְּיוֹם רָעָה)   *17:17*
                                          (יוֹם רָעָה)   17:18

In addition to this parallel tripartite structure, several themes occur throughout in both introduction and body. Echoes of the introduction's description of the uselessness of the nations' gods (B) sound not only in the corresponding section B', but also in the concluding section A'. In contrast to the nations' gods, YHWH, the well of living water, gives life. The concluding section cites the enemies' taunt concerning the delay of divine action or the plaintiff community's fervent wish that it may soon come ("Where is the word of the Lord?").[33] No divine oracle other than the introduction's claim that YHWH will make the nations to know his might "in this instant" (בַּפַּעַם הַזֹּאת אוֹדִיעֵם אֶת־יָדִי) occurs in the

---

[33]Cf. R. Carroll, *Jeremiah*, 362-64.

near context. Does the searching question, regardless of its origin and tenor, refer to the apparent delay of this instantaneous revolution in human affairs?

Granting the diverse backgrounds of the units which comprise Jer 16:19–17:18*, they have been crafted into a continuous composition with a sustained argument. A speaker, confident in YHWH's might and benevolence, predicts the day when even the nations will acknowledge the futility of their idol worship (16:19-20). In that moment (the return of the Exiles? of the Diaspora?), YHWH will make his might and name known to all (16:21). The issue of YHWH's willingness to relate to the nations in such a manner leads to a discussion of the gnomic principle of the benefits of trust properly placed. Anyone who trusts in human means faces failure; anyone who trusts in the one God will find sustenance (17:5-8). What of the distress of certain apparently righteous and the prosperity of certain apparently unrighteous individuals? From YHWH's perspective these apparent difficulties become questions of correct diagnosis (17:9-10) and patience (17:11). YHWH sees what no other can, the human heart; the principle of appropriate reward, however, may require time.

This argument also confronts a problem implicit throughout, although only rarely voiced in, the Jeremiah tradition, namely the Sodom and Gomorrah issue (see Abraham's petition, Genesis 18). Jer 15:1-4 relates the question to YHWH's final decision to punish because of Manasseh's sin. Regardless of the degree of guilt or innocence of the generation following Manasseh, YHWH's decision stands. Even Moses and Samuel, introduced apparently as examples of those, like Abraham, successful in reminding YHWH of his reputation for justice, will fail in any attempt to dissuade YHWH from his chosen course of action. Significantly, the issue does not seem to concern the possibility of *mercy for the guilty*. Forgiveness plays virtually no role in the book of Jeremiah. Just as Abraham sought justice from the Judge of All the Earth and Moses sought to protect YHWH's reputation, the people appeal to YHWH's reputation (Jer 14:7, 21) and the Jeremiah tradition attends especially to the question of the dependability of YHWH's character (Jer 31:35-37). If YHWH can be trusted to punish and reward any and all individuals with such fidelity, how does one understand, for example, the incidental disasters which befall the righteous when YHWH punishes the wicked? Surely some pious Jerusalemites suffered the common fate at the hands of the Babylonians. National judgment for national sins through the blunt instrument of an enemy nation's

invading army proves ill-suited for the individual justice described in Jer
17:5-13. The conclusion of this extended discussion in one of the so-
called "confessions" appropriately and poignantly addresses this concern:
"Heal me, YHWH, and I shall be healed . . . Do not become a terror to me
. . . Let my persecutors be shamed . . . let them be dismayed. . . . "

Characterization of Voices in the Dialogue

Four voices participate in this complex dialogue. An unidentified and
elusive individual or series of individuals (Jerusalem? Jeremiah? the nar-
rator/redactor/editor? some combination of these?) initiates the discussion.
Later YHWH, the community, and the nations (as cited in prospect by the
individual) join in the dialogue. These voices stand out in the book of
Jeremiah as expressions of issues implied in, but potentially subversive
to, the Jeremiah tradition. By virtue of its thematics and location at key
junctures, the dialogue, although a relatively inconspicuous topographical
feature, sounds a jarring countermelody to the main judgment-orthodoxy
theme of the book.

Individual

The opening statement in this discussion expresses a bitter, accusato-
ry plea for justice. It resignedly concedes that human beings have no control over their own fates. It implies that YHWH's punitive actions are, or
threaten to be, excessive—a harsh accusation in the context of the
Hebrew Bible. It suggests an alternative course of divine action. Frustra-
tion and fear give birth to vindictive, defensive displacement of anger.

This voice can only be characterized as a nonprophetic end-product
of prophetic logic. Resignation at fate growing from those components
of the tradition which pronounced certain judgment, mistrust of YHWH
arising from his unwillingness to forgive and his apparent blanket condemnation, and spiteful hatred toward the nations represent the darker
underside of prophetic religion. Remarkably, however, the discussion
attempts to resolve all of these flaws. The individual voice next appears
to reaffirm confidence in YHWH as the worshipper's source of strength and
deliverance and to announce the day when even the hated nations will
join Israel in worship of the one true God.

YHWH

The debate and its "resolution" manifest a central problem for radical ethical monotheism. Expectations of absolute divine justice for all individuals and all nations simply contradict human experience, modern and ancient. The contradiction, in turn, fundamentally challenges confidence in the deity. The discourse of the book of Jeremiah offers two common responses: (1) the one God's justice applies to the nations, as well, and (2) YHWH discerns the truth of guilt and innocence at a deeper level—the conflict is between appearance (experience) and reality, not between expectation and performance.

YHWH and the nations. The book of Jeremiah typically considers the nations simply as the instruments of YHWH's wrath. The nations have laid, or will lay, Israel waste (Jer 2:14-18; 4:7,20; 5:17; 8:16; 9:12; 20:4, 21:4,10,24-25; 28:14; 32:3-4; 34:21; 38:3,18); but these texts at least imply that the nations destroy at YHWH's behest. Interestingly, while well over half of the prose references to this destructive agency, specifically Babylon, adopt this straightforward stance, others go on to deal with the problem of Babylon's responsibility over against Israel. These texts include warnings to Babylon which seem almost to contradict depictions of Babylon and its king as YHWH's servant. They maintain that, although Babylon is YHWH's agent in a judgment inescapable for Judah, Babylon, too, will experience its season of pain (Jer 25:12-14; 27:7; 29:10-12).

The sentiment of these texts finds a parallel in two isolated texts and a cluster of passages in the oracles against the nations (10:25; 30:15-16;[34] 50:17-18,33-34; 51:24,34-35,49). A bitterness toward those who have harmed YHWH's uniquely chosen marks these texts. They have criminally

---

[34]Jer 30:15 almost contradicts its context. After a statement of Israel's culpability and the justice of her plight, 30:16 announces that "therefore" all those who have devoured her will be devoured! This contrasts sharply with the kindred notion expressed in Jer 2:3 to the effect that in his early days Israel was protected from all those who sought to devour him, but that now his guilt has moved YHWH to withdraw protection. Jer 2:3 argues that Israel's sheltered status among the nations has been endangered by its sin; Jer 30:16 offers this protection despite its sin. Commonalities of language do not equate with unity of position. Jeremiah 2–3 and 30–31, while obviously very closely related, may be overhastily identified with one another.

violated YHWH's inheritance. Furthermore, they have sinned against YHWH by arrogantly and gleefully plundering YHWH's heritage without realizing that they, too, are subject to his judgment (46:15,25; 48:7,13,26-30,42-44; 49:1-6,16:50:14,24,32; 51:44,52). Only Jer 3:17, 12:14-17, and 16:19-21 treat the possibility of conversion for the nations. The nations themselves, so much a topic of discussion in the dialogue, speak once, briefly, in citation. They voice a monotheistic polemic against idolatry in the style of Jer 10:1-16.

YHWH and the Individual. YHWH's response to objections against the propriety of his judgment receive greater attention. YHWH, or the individual speaking on YHWH's behalf, takes great pains to defend YHWH's reputation for justice. This defense attains even greater weight through links with the prophetic "confessions" and will be discussed in detail below.

Community

Interestingly, the individual voice which began this dialogue gives place to the voice of the community beginning in Jer 14:19-22. Initially, the community expresses the terror and dismay characteristic of the community elsewhere in the book of Jeremiah. Like the individual voice in Jer 10:23-25, the community voice appeals for YHWH's fidelity to his standards of justice—his promsies and his covenant. The community confesses its sin and pleads for forgiveness. Finally, the community expresses its monotheistic convictions in an anti-idolatry polemic similar, once again, to that of Jer 10:1-16.

The issues raised plaintively in Jer 14:19-22 resurface later in two statements by or to the community. Jer 17:12-13 concludes the explication of YHWH's just response to individual guilt and innocence, specifically according to the criterion of trust in YHWH. Here the community doxologizes YHWH as sanctuary and hope and confesses that those who have, in fact, abandoned YHWH deserve their fate. In effect, the community acquiesces, yielding to the argument that YHWH's actions are just when measured by the "private" criteria of trust in YHWH and the intentions of the will.

The community concludes (Jer 20:13) in response to a call to praise. YHWH has, in fact, behaved in accordance with the expectations of orthodoxy—he has delivered the innocent. Since guilt and innocence are not always subject to public determination, the community chooses to trust YHWH.

Summary

In sum, then, the discussion "matures." All challenges inherent in the opening statement in the individual voice are met. YHWH acts justly. The nations do, indeed, play a role in YHWH's plan. The innocent have, in fact, been delivered.

Contours of the Dialogue: Implications for the Composition and Genre of the Book of Jeremiah

Observations concerning the structure of Jer 16:19–17:18* seem to explain the unusual form of 16:19-21, that is, it was constructed as the introduction to an extended compositional unit made up of a number of originally discrete components. This conclusion also offers solutions to other problems. The speaker of 16:19 may be identified with the speaker of 17:14-18 and the *relative* secondary nature of 17:1-4 seems confirmed. The reference to the delayed fulfillment of YHWH's word probably refers to the oracle concerning the universal establishment of YHWH's justice and reputation, for example. The hypothesis that the concerns and techniques of the redactional effort responsible for the "liturgical" materials currently under discussion may be most transparently studied in 16:19–17:18 seems also to have proven tenable.

On the other hand, a new series of questions arises. In terms of proportion and scholarly attention received, the deuteronomistic prose, the presumably authentic oracles of judgment, and the prophetic "confessions" dominate Jeremiah 7–20. If, however, the materials examined in this chapter may properly be read together and if their distribution across 7–20 suggests a significant structural role, Jeremiah scholarship has overlooked a major voice in the final composition of the book. Does the polemic against idols in Jer 10:1-16 take on new significance on the structural level as integral to a near-final redaction of the book of Jeremiah? Should the "prophetic liturgy" of Jeremiah 14 be seen in a similar new light? Indeed, the analysis presented above indicates that the "confessions," themselves, should be seen, not as governing structures, but as elements finally subsumed into the argument of this fundamentally theological redaction.

As R. Carroll noted,[35] the material analyzed above does not focus on the concerns of the early Jeremiah tradition. Moving beyond the national crisis confronting a sinful nation whose God punishes for infidelity, even beyond subsequent interests in the recuperation of the relationship and the return of the nation's exiles, this material addresses universal questions: one God relating in one way to all people individually, with subtlety, nuance, and precision. Furthermore, read cumulatively, this material treats these questions as fundamental theological problems raised, in part, by the interests of earlier stages in the development of the tradition. YHWH's wholesale punishment raised the issue of his justice to individual members of the elect; the use of foreign armies as the tool of punishment raised the question of YHWH's relationship to foreign sinners; YHWH's *Ausschliesslichkeitsanspruch* suggested equally radical claims that the "judge of all the world do justice" (Gen 18:25).

Exegetes often focus on questions of the authenticity and text of Jer 10:1-16 to the exclusion of questions of macrostructural function.[36] Its sharp polemic, not in full agreement with materials in subsequent portions of the book (esp. 12:14-17; 16:19-21),[37] probably reflects the divergent origins of these materials. From the perspective of the final form of the book, however, Jeremiah 10:1-16 interjects a problem which becomes a focus for the remainder of the collection, namely the fact that the worship of any god other than YHWH contradicts his absolute sovereignty. Its language generates a series of responses (see "learn the way of the nations," 10:2; "Who would not fear you, O king of the nations?" 10:7; "the nations cannot endure his indignation," 10:10; "He makes lightnings for the rain," 10:13; "their images are . . . worthless, a work of delusion," 10:14-15), organized, in the final form of the book, into a logical, well-developed discussion.

The so-called "prophetic liturgy" of Jeremiah 14 plays a similar role. Scholars, reading Jeremiah 14 without attention to its role in the larger

---

[35] *Jeremiah*, 353.

[36] J. Thompson (*Jeremiah*, 126) describes Jeremiah 7–10 in terms of the theme of "false religion and its punishment," thereby calling attention to connections between Jer 10:1-16 and the idolatry topos in the Temple Sermon.

[37] Cf. the comments of R. Carroll (*Jeremiah*, 254-58) and W. McKane (*Jeremiah*, 216-28).

context, focus attention on its historical setting in the prophet's life and ministry.[38] Did the people's repentance fail? Was it hypothetical or disingenuous? Like 10:1-16, Jeremiah 14 contains material which predates the redaction responsible for the final form of Jer 16:19–17:18*. In contrast to the universalistic thrust of 16:19-21, for example, Jeremiah 14 expresses purely nationalistic sentiments. Again, from the perspective of the final form of the text, however, Jeremiah 14 provides language which can later be transformed for new uses and serve as a foil for the advancement of the discussion, as well. This juxtaposition of materials through interconnective allusion culminates, then, in a difficult doxology praising YHWH as the one who "delivers the soul of the needy" (Jer 20:13). In light of the editorial processes observable, particularly in 16:19–17:18*, this doxology, couched amid the complaints of an exemplary righteous sufferer, represents the voice of late piety.

This "liturgical" redaction, then, does not primarily concern national crisis, national deity, or national punishment. Neither does it address the fate of one individual prophet only, not even as the representative of the collective. Jer 17:14-18, whatever its origin, has been subsumed and transformed into a problematization of YHWH's ability to act justly on the level of the righteous individual. The "confessions" challenge YHWH to distinguish the righteous individual from the surrounding evildoers. They call YHWH to faithfulness to his reputation as sole God, able to know the human heart, and just to requite according to deeds.

Finally, heard with other "voices" in Jeremiah 7–20, this liturgical scheme raises the hermeneutical question of genre for the book of Jeremiah as a whole. If, besides presumably authentic poetry and the prose tradition of the book, Jeremiah preserves several other voices—for example, the voice of the postcrisis worshiping community, the voice of a tradition of truly theological reflection—how should the book, as a whole, be read? Clearly more than an anthology of prophetic oracles, the book may not be adequately described as a collection of materials by, about, and in the tradition of the prophet Jeremiah. A formative stage in the composition of the book has shaped it in such a way as to guide the reader to consider questions of YHWH's justice, not just for grossly unfaith-

---

[38]Cf. the ingenious interpretation of W. Holladay (*Jeremiah*, 427-29), who assigns the very specific date November/December 601 BCE.

ful nations, but for the isolated righteous individual interspersed within the unfaithful community. The message of Jeremiah the prophet and the confirmation of his message through the events of the Babylonian crisis, become more than authoritative. They are also provocative, problematical. The book of Jeremiah—like the books of Isaiah, Ezekiel, and the Twelve—has been given pedagogical functions by those who gave it final shape.

Conclusions

In the precritical era of interpretation, scholars regarded prophetic books as the literary product of "writing" prophets. Interpreters emphasized one voice, that of the prophetic author, throughout. During the dominance of the source-critical and form-critical methods, prophetic books were regarded as anthologies of short, originally oral, oracles which had attracted a variety of "secondary" or "inauthentic" accretions. Scholars were preoccupied with reconstructing the "original" voice, which they presumed to have uttered discrete, disjointed sayings. Newer literary critics, dubious of historical reconstructions and interested in synchronous readings, choose, in effect, to regard prophetic books as fictive literary products. In a "second naiveté" of sorts, they choose to disregard often overwhelming evidence of the composite nature of prophetic literature in favor of a stategy of reading which threatens to force homogeneity on the literature.

In contrast to these approaches, the method employed above seeks to attend primarily to voices and characterizations *as defined and presented in the text*. The attempt has been made to recognize the complex literary history of Jeremiah while care has been taken not to prejudice the literary integrity *of the text*. The effort has been made to allow each voice produced by the tradition to speak in *its distinctive manner*.

Voice and Polyphony

Jeremiah preserves a virtual chorus of voices in dialogue, some presumably contemporaneous with one another, some from widely dispersed historical and social settings. The phenomenon of voice as observed in Jeremiah requires a sophisticated interpretive model, since several literary tropes can be and are often easily confused with one another. The phenomenon described by the term "voice" here is not simply synonymous with a grammatical category (a shift from third-person-plural to second-person-singular forms of address, for example). Neither are metaphor and simile sufficient descriptions of the phenomenon. The "voice" of Lady Zion in the book of Jeremiah operates on a higher level than statements such as "Jerusalem is like a woman" (simile) and "Jerusalem is childless" (metaphor). In such cases, a poet describes some aspect of Jerusalem "objectively" (as an object), albeit symbolically. On the other hand, when Mother Jerusalem cries, "Woe is me, I faint before murderers!" she speaks as a subject. In such cases, a poet has given Jerusalem literary independence. She is no longer simply the object of discussion but a subjective participant in dialogue with other participants. She is a character with a voice of her own.

An Aid to Interpretation of Characters

This awareness of the independence of "voices" in prophetic literature can enrich interpretive possibilities along two axes. First, biblical authors frequently employ "cultural commonplaces" or matrices of concepts, tropes, and language with long histories in the tradition.[1] As a result, language, both figurative (such as personification) and nonfigurative,[2] that alludes to or employs elements of one of these cultural matrices invokes an entire constellation of concepts and conventions. By appropriating these "cultural commonplaces," prophetic literature often produces "voices" with greater depth of character than can be discerned from analysis limited to a given specimen of language that appears in the text. By grounding the voice in the stream of tradition, biblical authors often provide figures with extensive identities.

Second, the concept of "voice" itself allows for an invaluable distinction between the literary figure and the author/redactor. In their present orchestration, "voices" in the book of Jeremiah enter into discussions pertinent to themes that confronted "post-Jeremianic" Judah. They address these issues on various levels, from sometimes radically divergent theological and traditional perspectives, and certainly in distinctive styles. As literary characters, these voices are the creations of authors. Nonbiblical literary critics evaluate the qualities of literature on the basis of the

---

[1]K. Darr, *Isaiah's Vision*, 36-45.

[2]The argument could be made that the prophets contain predominantly figurative language, especially that all speech by or about YHWH is figurative. In a sense, by giving YHWH a voice biblical authors personify YHWH. This phenomenon manifests itself, e.g., in the various portrayals of YHWH in the book of Jeremiah.

independence, credibility, and complexity of literary characters.[3] In a real sense, elements of prophetic literature are equally fictional characterizations. As a personification, Lady Jerusalem is a fictional character. The community, too, is a "fictional" entity. What is the relationship between the "real" community and the literary "voice"? What is the relationship between the community "voice" and the author/redactor's own position? Descriptions of the former relationship are limited by the stereotypical data provided by the commonplace allusion. Descriptions of the latter relationship are limited to data implied in the situation that can be presumed to have motivated the author to utilize a given "voice."

Nevertheless, rather than hopelessly obscuring the historical context of the authors/redactors, the voices they choose reveal a great deal, if not about the identities of the authors/redactors, certainly about their theological/traditional convictions and social settings. At least four examples of this grounding in cultural commonplaces and theological traditions occur in the Jeremiah material analyzed above.

The Community. When the community speaks in the book of Jeremiah, it speaks almost exclusively as the desperate confessing/lamenting congregation. Its voice is the cry for YHWH's assistance and fidelity to his promises and covenant. Firmly grounded in the tradition of confession and lament, it expresses dismay that YHWH has not responded as in ages past to the community's plea for deliverance. The community voices reaction to crisis.

The Prophet. The prophetic voice raises issues associated on a canonical level with the Abraham-Moses-Samuel tradition of prophetic concern for YHWH's reputation as righteous judge. The "commonplace" is neither the notion of the prophet as representative of the people *to* the deity (an "intercessor" theme of divine mercy and forgiveness) nor the traditional notion of the prophet as the representative of the deity *to* the people (a "spokesperson" or "messenger"). The prophet is a very different kind of "representative" of the deity, as his complaints all reflect the concern that YHWH be proven just.

Lady Jerusalem. Perhaps the most striking example of the rich texture provided by association with a cultural commonplace involves the personification of Lady Jerusalem. Commentators who simply note shifts to

---

[3]Keats respected Shakespeare for his "negative capability."

feminine-singular verbal forms as demarcations of units or who analyze feminine passages in the book of Jeremiah as isolated metaphors fail to recognize the significant relationship between these texts and a well-established ancient Near Eastern and biblical literary technique of personifying capital and leading cities as goddesses (extrabiblical); consorts of the deity (extrabiblical, but see Isa 62:5); and, above all, mothers of their inhabitants (Jer 10:19-20; Isa 62:1-5, to name only two of many biblical examples).[4]

In the book of Jeremiah, this trope functions specifically in two ways. YHWH addresses Lady Zion charging her with infidelity and warning her that she will be abandoned, exposed, desecrated, humiliated, and murdered.[5] Lady Zion, herself, speaks only in cries of despair and mourning. These exchanges, then, engender an impression of immediacy—an angry and cuckolded deity, a frightened and imperiled spouse and mother. Notably, Lady Zion offers no defense of her actions, either by way of excuse or explanation. She merely reacts to her fate. Whether by calculated intent or as an expression of an immediate context of crisis, the dialogue between YHWH and Lady Zion merits appreciation for its dramatic, violent, and emotive force. Aside from the assertion, central to the Jeremiah tradition, that Jerusalem brought her fate upon herself, the dialogue is not highly theological. The tasks of theological evaluation, assessment, and commentary belong to other strands of discourse in the book.

YHWH. YHWH participates in virtually all of the dialogues in the book and, consequently, receives several distinct characterizations related to various tradition-matrices. YHWH is, by implication (that is, in the eyes of the community), the deliverer of the Exodus and Judges traditions. YHWH responds, however, as the frustrated God of the Covenant whose patience long ago reached its limits. Because of Judah's history of sin (especially during the reign of Manasseh) and because the contemporary generation continues unabated in this sin, does not recognize inconsistencies between its behavior and the Covenant, and exhibits no predilection for YHWH's word, YHWH announces his decision, reached before Jeremiah's ministry begins, to punish. Significantly, the nearest biblical analogues to this

---

[4]See Darr, *Isaiah's Vision*, esp. 124-204.

[5]See the discussions of the dynamics of this language in J. Galambush, *Jerusalem*, 4-24 and K. Darr, *Isaiah's Vision*, 113-23.

decision—the Flood, the destruction of Sodom and Gomorrah, the punishment of the Wandering generation, the rejection of Saul, the destruction of Shiloh, and, of course, the destruction and conquest of Samaria—do not serve prophetic rhetoric to the degree, for example, that Exodus and Covenant traditions do. In fact, the relation to the tradition established by references to "intercession," and especially to Moses and Samuel, contributes to the problematization of divine justice voiced by the community in the "liturgical" materials and by the prophet in the "confessions." In other instances when YHWH reached definitive decisions to punish, he provided a means of survival for the righteous (retrospectively, Noah, Lot, a later generation of innocents, David, the preservation of the Ark, even a Samarian remnant). Will (/has) YHWH make (/made) the same provision for the innocent in the Babylonian crisis? YHWH addresses this problem in a third dialogue (with the prophet?) concerning the subtlety and nuance of divine justice. In this discourse, YHWH reflects the character of the abstract wisdom and theological traditions in the Hebrew Bible.

Discourse Structures

Canonical status may by nature require, and certainly reflects de facto, the inclusion of such variety. Authors and traditionists seem to have valued variety of viewpoints and to have resisted the temptation to resolve complex issues simplistically or to dissolve tensions in perspective. Two types of discourse structuring frame the materials analyzed above.

The early portions of the book employ mainly short units of poetic speech arranged in sometimes extended dialogues comprising rapid, almost staccato exchanges between participants. Introductory formulae, narrative frameworks, and other discourse markers appear only rarely. While the temptation to regard this technique as "earlier"[6] may be true

---

[6]This viewpoint is an often implicit assumption of scholars who argue for a roughly chronological arrangement of the book of Jeremiah, with the earlier preaching of Jeremiah gathered toward the beginning of the book. Interestingly, this technique characterizes Jeremiah 4–6 and, to a lesser degree, Jeremiah 3. Jeremiah 2, on the other hand, exhibits a much greater frequency of explicit discourse markers and, relatedly, a much better developed overall structure. As is the case in the prose material, a dominant speaker, YHWH, controls and directs the discussion in Jeremiah 2 (and 3). Other speakers, notably the community and

in relative terms, the primary distinction over against the technique employed beginning in Jeremiah 7 seems to be related to the transition in theme from the people's reaction to catastrophe (Jeremiah 4–6) to YHWH's deliberations and pain (Jeremiah 7–14).

The prose-dominated portions of the book, beginning with the Temple Sermon in Jeremiah 7, exhibit an entirely different mode or discourse. Here, the discourse proceeds in highly structured, multilayered narrative. Whereas the poetry fostered an impression of energetic engagement, reaction and counterreaction to a crisis situation, the prose is very deliberate. Reading Jeremiah 4–6, one can envision a busy stage full of characters (YHWH, Lady Zion, the prophet, the people, the Babylonians, the watchman blowing alarm); the prose narratives involve only YHWH and the prophet in private audience.

Prominence, Character, and Role of Certain Voices

Somewhat surprisingly, regardless of the structuring technique, the voice of the prophet does not carry the melody in the ensemble. Instead, the tradition expresses a strong tendency to present the words contained in the book of Jeremiah as divine speech. The community voices its pain and desperation in the laments characteristic of Jeremiah 4–10; it raises the issue of divine justice in the "liturgical" conversation in Jeremiah 10–20; and the prophet joins this controversy in the prophetic complaints. Throughout, however, the voice of YHWH provides the thematic, controlling perspective.

The Book of Jeremiah as YHWH Speech

The final form of Jeremiah (MT) tends toward a depiction of the entire book as YHWH speech in a manner which produces a relative "absence" of the prophet. In this regard, the book of Jeremiah exhibits characteristics similar to those observed by C. Seitz concerning the book of Isaiah. Seitz notes that in the final form of Isaiah, "God does most of the talking," resulting in a "retraction of the prophetic persona."[7] The analy-

---

Lady Jerusalem, are heard only as cited by YHWH.

[7]"Isaiah 1–66: Making Sense of the Whole," in *Reading and Preaching the Book of Isaiah*, ed. C. Seitz (Philadelphia: Fortress Press, 1988) 121.

sis above has identified two phenomena, especially prominent in MT, that contribute to this tendency in the book of Jeremiah.

On a microcontextual level, the tradition often explicitly attributes individual units to YHWH. Interpreters operating on form-critical assumptions (someone, presumably the prophet, spoke these units; the genre involved had social settings) or pragmatic considerations (the content or sentiment of these units is inappropriate for the deity) have tended to ignore the express contention of the text. Nevertheless, the regularity with which the text asserts that YHWH speaks these units represents an intentional literary strategy.

This phenomenon occurs particularly in Jeremiah 8–9, 14, and 17. Although MT and LXX agree in marking divine speech at several points (8:4, 13; 9:6, 8, 11, 14, 16, 19, 22, 24), MT amplifies its portrayal of the divine laments in Jeremiah 8 through additional markers at five key points (8:17; 9:2, 5, 21). MT and LXX concur that Jer 14:17 introduces divine speech; MT alone identifies YHWH as the speaker (v 5) of the subsequent wisdom psalm in Jer 17:5-11. Clearly, the evidence does not support the conclusion that MT and LXX differ qualitatively regarding the tendency to attribute to YHWH the preponderance of sayings in the book. Instead, the distinction seems to be quantitative in nature. Given the obvious insistence of the tradition that YHWH spoke the sayings in question, interpretation of the book of Jeremiah should honor the text. The text demonstrates little or no concern for the "original" setting of these sayings. The canonical book conveys the word of YHWH. YHWH speaks. YHWH even laments the destruction of his people.

On a macrocontextual level, incipits that structure the final form of the book (Jer 1:1-3; 3:6; 7:1-3; 11:1-3; 14:1; among others) go a step farther to subsume entire discourses under the heading of YHWH speech. In a complicated and sophisticated literary conceit, these incipits set discourses such as the Temple Sermon in the realm of private communication between YHWH and the prophet. In these discourses, YHWH details verbatim exchanges in which the prophet will be involved: YHWH not only states the message to be delivered but also anticipates responses from Jeremiah's audience, dictates Jeremiah's counterresponse, and deals with Jeremiah's own objections.

From the standpoint of the canonical status and composition history of the book, perhaps the most interesting feature of these discourses involves the fact that they exhibit little concern with the oral delivery of the prophetic word in its "original" public setting. Instead, they seem to be consciously aware that the primary audience of these discourses will be the book's readership. In them the readership hears the underlying voice of the narrator who shares perspectives and insights that would have presumably been inaccessible to the "original" audience (and in some cases perhaps even to the prophet). The narrator/redactor responsible for shaping these discourses is aware, for example, of the outcome of Jeremiah's ministry and of the aftermath of its crisis setting. The narrator/redactor knows that YHWH's decision regarding the fate of Judah was reached even before Jeremiah's ministry began. In the view of the narrator/redactor, Jeremiah, as a prophet privy to the divine council, must have also known.

This consciousness already underlies the introduction to the entire book (Jer 1:1-3) and the opening discourse (the so-called "call narrative," Jer 1:4-19). The superscription not only conforms stylistically to the incipits that head discourses later in the book, but, in both MT and LXX versions, it seems more interested in describing the book as the "Word of YHWH" (1:1, LXX; 1:2, LXX and MT) than as the "words of Jeremiah" (1:1, MT only).[8] The "call narrative" itself reports a quintessential example of "private" communication between YHWH and the prophet. According

---

[8] Superscriptions to prophetic books can be classed in three common categories (Nah 1:1; Hab 1:1; and Mal 1:1 are each unique): "the words of PN" (Amos 1:1); "the vision of PN [which he saw]" (Isa 1:1; Obad 1); "the word of YHWH which was to PN" (Hos 1:1; Joel 1:1; Mic 1:1; Zeph 1:1; cf Jon 1:1; Hag 1:1; Zech 1:1). Jer 1:1 seems to be a conflation of the first and third types. LXX represents an expanded version of the third, most common, type. Several scholars have seen the conflation and the LXX variant as evidence that the superscription has been secondarily expanded in MT, arguing either for the priority of vv 1, 3 (so F. Horst, "Die Anfänge des Propheten Jeremia," ZAW 41 [1923]: 98-99) or for the priority of v 1a alone (so W. Thiel, Redaktion, 55-57). Others (B. Duhm, Jeremia, 4; J. Thompson, Jeremiah, 139-41) see no reason to conclude that this obviously editorial heading has undergone expansion. The text-critical issue has no bearing on the argument that the introduction, in both MT and LXX, emphasizes that the book contains the "Word of YHWH." For a thorough summary of scholarly discussion of textual and historical questions raised by the superscription see J. Lundbom, The Early Career of the Prophet Jeremiah (Lewiston NY: Mellen, 1993).

to this account, YHWH reveals to the prophet both the futility of the ministry he will undertake (in the sense that the people will not respond) and the extreme opposition and hostility the prophet will encounter. The tonalities of YHWH's voice, the awareness of the determined outcome, and the presumption that the prophet was aware of what lay ahead from the outset necessarily condition any competent reading of the book.[9]

The Significance of "Minor" Dialogues

The "artificiality" and limitations of this "Word of YHWH" principle are readily apparent in relation to the "liturgical" voice in Jeremiah 10–20. Whether because of limitations inherent in the conceit that the entire contents of the book are the Word of YHWH, because the more consistent examples of this technique occur in freely composed prose, or because some "miscellaneous" materials postdate the redaction responsible for the basic macrostructure of the book, a variety of units situated toward the end of blocks demarcated by incipits do not fit into the "Word of YHWH" conceit. Jer 10:1 and 14:1, for example, both depict the sections they head as Word of YHWH (respectively, "Hear the word which YHWH speaks to you . . . "; "The word of YHWH which came to Jeremiah concerning . . . "). Yet both introduce dialogues involving, principally, YHWH, the worshipping community, and the prophet. In both cases, the units that follow abandon YHWH speech within six verses. These dialogues cohere around a common theme and common language, not under the organizing influence of a narrative voice.

Another function of the voices in these dialogues merits comment. A competent reader of the book, aware of the book's sequence, will become aware that texts situated in several of these local dialogues share vocabulary, themes, and viewpoints. In fact, specific statements often find their complements, not in the immediate context, but much later.

---

[9]The impact on the reader, particularly the ancient reader, achieved by the foregrounding of these perspectives cannot be overestimated. Reading is a fundamentally sequential act and, as K. Darr points out (*Isaiah's Vision*, 28-30, 230n.17), scrolls simply must be read sequentially. As the narrator/redactor responsible for Jeremiah 1 (and apparently Jeremiah 7, 11, etc.) knew, ancient readers of the book of Jeremiah would have been well aware of the literary sequence of the book.

The objection and plea voiced by an individual worshipper in Jer 10:23-25 in a particularly charged and poignant cry, for example, remains largely unanswered until Jer 12:14-17. Of three issues broached in this plea, the questions of YHWH's relationship to the righteous individual and of YHWH's ability to discern the inner life of an individual receive attention in the intervening materials (Jer 11:18–12:6). But the intervening prophetic "confession(s)" do not presuppose that YHWH has punished the speaker as does the complaint in Jer 10:23-25. Furthermore, YHWH responds to the indignant, bitter, and accusatorial suggestion that he punish the nations (if he must punish someone) *only* in Jer 12:14-17 and, subsequently, in Jer 16:19-21. In a parallel manner, the admission that the nations' gods are "nothings" in Jer 14:22 also finds its complement in Jer 16:19-21. Similarities in language and theme, especially concerning the issues of idol polemic and "learning" in the sense of conversion, are unmistakable.

In Jer 17:5-13 and Jer 20:13 the discussion returns to the other major theme initiated in Jer 10:23-25, namely the problem of YHWH's just treatment of the righteous individual, so that this theme forms an inclusio around the whole.[10] Just as the human dialogue partner progresses from anger (10:25) to confession of YHWH's exclusive deity (14:23) to a doxology praising YHWH as the one who will elicit similar confessions even from the nations (16:19-20) in the first part of the dialogue, the human partner moves from near-cynicism (10:12-24) to confession of sin (14:20) and of YHWH's righteousness (17:12-13) and, finally, to call on others to praise YHWH as deliverer of the individual (20:13) in the second.

Book-Level Implications

Finally, the analysis offered above gives rise to a number of summary conclusions and observations: (1) The literary shape of the final form of

---

[10]The composite, bipartite character of Jer 10:23-25 may be significant in relation to this inclusio. Jer 10:23-24, which quotes a proverb, occurs first and links with the closing wisdom treatment of the relationship between YHWH and the righteous Everperson. Jer 10:25, which quotes a psalm of communal lament, links with the internal communal lament discussions of YHWH, Israel, and the nations. Jer 10:23-25 seems to have been composed as the "theme statement" of this bipartite structure.

the book produces a voice remarkably removed from the realm of prophecy, understood in the conventional sense as the ministry of an individual spokesperson for the deity in a specific historical and cultural context. (2) The baroque manner in which the final form of the book incorporates given literary units in multiple relationships lends the book a polyphonic, even contrapuntal character. (3) The question of the genre of prophetic books, like its counterpart in Gospels research, remains a largely unresolved problem.

Literary Shape and Narrative Voice

The phenomena of unexpected attribution of specific units to YHWH and the extended divine discourses delivered privately to the prophet participate in an even broader literary phenomenon in the book of Jeremiah. To borrow a term from narratology, the "implied author"[11] of Jeremiah 1–20, indeed of the whole book, displays virtual omniscience. The narrator responsible for structuring Jeremianic voices in dialogue: knows the mind of YHWH; can report private exchanges between YHWH and Jeremiah; speaks for the community and Lady Zion; is fully cognizant of the final outcome of the Babylonian crisis; knows the issues which (will) face exilic and postexilic Judah; and so on.

To be sure, this near-omniscience is an artifact of the redaction and composition history of the book, as is generally recognized. The remarkable feature of the book, however, is—contrary to conventional readings—the relative scarcity of materials which give clear evidence of the historical prophet's perspective. Virtually all YHWH's speeches, both prose and poetry, address issues which presume the outcome of the prophet's career. Even the prophet's complaints voice questions concerning divine justice, not the expected and much-sought-after expressions of prophetic

---

[11]This term is virtually indistiguishable from "final redactor(s)." It is useful, here, because of the persistence of theories which presume a strong "prophetic" involvement in the production of a final or semifinal form of some portion of the book. The notion that Jeremiah 1–20, or substantial portions of it, was given final form by the prophet himself (the implied author) cannot withstand comparison to a "profile" of this author. Instead, a description of the "implied author" of Jeremiah 1–20 very closely resembles a redaction critic's description of a final redactor, quite distant from the prophet in time and outlook.

disappointment and sympathy for his people. They, too, presume the outcome.

In the end, it becomes extremely difficult to persist in the assumption that the book of Jeremiah exhibits any interest in a "historical" presentation of the career and preaching of the "historical" Jeremiah. Its complex structure does not reflect the stratigraphy of its growth such that authentic materials appear in pristine condition early in the book with accretions concentrated later. "Authentic" kernels of Jeremianic preaching cannot be reliably distilled using metrical or stylistic criteria. Diachronic analyses of the book must work back from a final form produced by a canonical interest in decontextualizing; synchronic analyses must take seriously the fact that the book, itself, does not confuse the narrative voice (= the final redactor[s]) with the prophetic.

In effect, on the book level, Jeremiah presents a theology of history rather than a prophetic theology. From a retrospective vantage point, the final form of the book comments on the Babylonian crisis as YHWH's plan, determined from the outset although in great anguish, the prophet's role as privy councilor, the subtlety of YHWH's system of justice, and, briefly, the international scope of YHWH's order. The de-emphasis of Jeremiah's actual preaching ministry is particularly evident in the prose treatment of repentance as a merely theoretical possibility and in the preoccupation with various aspects of the problem of theodicy raised by YHWH's decision to punish and YHWH's method in executing the punishment. The "confessions" of Jeremiah participate in this theodicy; they do not reflect a biographical crisis of despair. Instead, given the fact that the book assumes that Jeremiah knew the outcome from the beginning of his ministry, the "confessions" portray a prophet eager for the execution of the divine verdict, on the one hand. Given the potential for unselective punishment at the hands of the Babylonians, the "confessions" portray a prophet troubled for YHWH's reputation, on the other. These concerns exhibit a certain consonance with other portions of the prophetic corpus. The books of Isaiah and Ezekiel, for example, both represent a theology of history which depicts the prophets as more-or-less fully informed of final outcomes (Isaiah 6; Ezek 3:1-11). The Dodecapropheton also incorporates a historical hermeneutic which addresses issues raised by the outcomes of the Assyrian and Babylonian crises rather than a historical record of the preaching of prophetic figures.[12] Like Jeremiah, the other prophetic books contain messages that, in the final analysis, offer only the theoretical possibility of repentance.

Polyphonic Argumentation

The analysis offered above encountered a variety of intertextual phenomena, also presumably the result of the redaction and composition history of the book, that require special attention in the task of interpretation. Several passages participate in multiple structures. Preexisting units were apparently appropriated as components of new "dialogues" by later editors through editorial linkages and allusions.

Jeremiah 14 provides a prime example of this phenomenon. It can be read as a self-contained unit. The communal laments link it with the broader lament tradition in the book (Jer 3:21-25, for example). The divine laments allude to divine laments elsewhere, and especially in Jeremiah 8–9, or vice versa. The collocation of lament, idol polemic, and language common to the "liturgical" codae in Jeremiah 10 and 16 bring it into the discussions of divine pain and divine justice which form threads across Jeremiah 7–20.[13] Read in continuity with Jeremiah 15–17, it participates in the discussion of the role of the prophet in preaching to an already doomed people (Jer 15:1-4; 16:19–17:13*). In essence, Jeremiah 14 can be described as a major nexus in Jeremiah 1–20. Most, if not all, threads of the discussion pass through this single chapter.

The Problem of Genre

Finally, these observations resurrect an issue which deserves renewed attention. What is a prophetic book? Historical criticism has conventionally responded to this question with descriptions and analyses of prophetic preaching, understood as orally delivered smaller units designed to address the immediate contexts of listening audiences. This preaching, it has been argued, intended to produce changes in the behavior of its

---

[12]See, e.g., the discussion in J. Nogalski, *Redactional Processes in the Book of the Twelve*, BZAW 218 (New York: Walter de Gruyter, 1993) 141-42, 210-12, 274-80.

[13]Linkages between Jeremiah 8, 10, and 14 are particularly striking. See, e.g., Jer 8:19 ‖ 10:3, 8, 14, 15 ‖ 14:22; Jer 8:20 ‖ 10:25 ‖ 14:6, 9, 12; Jer 8:21 ‖ 10:19 ‖ 14:17; and, esp. Jer 8:23 ‖ 14:17, 18.

audience: to avert disaster or to motivate faith responses to hopeful new situations. As a corrective to older views of prophecy this conventional approach has undeniable merit. As an assessment of the current book of Jeremiah in its entirety, however, this solution is inadequate. The book presumes outcomes, degrades specific contextual references, and downplays the individual, historical Jeremiah. In short, it functions on a canonical level—offering the paradigmatic word of YHWH to the community of faith for all time and in all settings. Conceptually, it is *several steps removed* from the career of the prophet. It deals in abstractions, retrospections, and theological reflections. Its dominant voices are those of YHWH and a theological narrator/redactor/commentator while it sets a multitude of other voices in dialogue with one another.

How can the book of Jeremiah be described generically? How should it be interpreted in light of its genre? It is neither a biography nor a mere anthology of the prophet's preaching. The question of genre cannot be settled here, but two contemporary analogues suggest themselves as aids for understanding certain generic features of Jeremiah.

First, the book of Jeremiah bears a certain resemblance to interpretive case studies: it contains select citations (whether "authentic" or no) of the prophet and other figures set, in the final form, in a metadiscursive framework. It examines perspectives *about* the significance of the preaching of Jeremiah, the response to that preaching, and the outcome of the crisis. Like modern analytical historiography, except, of course, for the strong theological assumptions, it champions an interpretation of history. It invites its readers to extrapolate historical trends into their present. Theologically, it encourages speculation concerning the will and purposes of God beyond the specific events in the sixth century BCE.

Second, the book of Jeremiah exhibits a degree of "hypertextuality." It models a wide variety of positions and responses. Voices, themes, and vocabulary appear to reappear later. Like sophisticated symphony audiences, sophisticated readers of the book of Jeremiah will discern the linkages and interplay, the dialogue. Jeremiah resists simple consecutive reading strategies. In the final analysis, Jeremiah is remarkably and acutely open-ended. It refuses to look only to the specific past. It encourages readers to read again, to listen again for a voice or theme or interplay unheard in the first reading.

Bibliography

Books

Ahuis, F. *Der Klagende Gerichtsprophet: Studien zur Klage in der Überlieferung von der altestamentlichen Gerichtspropheten*. Stuttgart: Calwer, 1982.

Bak, D. *Klagender Gott—klagende Menschen: Studien zur Klage im Jeremia-buch*, BZAW 193. New York: Walter de Gruyter, 1990.

Baumgartner, W. *Die Klagegedichte des Jeremia*. Giessen: Alfred Töpelmann, 1917.

Bellinger, W. *A Hermeneutic of Curiosity and Readings of Psalm 61*. SOTI 1. Macon GA: Mercer University Press, 1995.

Berridge, J. *Prophet, People, and Word of Yahweh: An Examination of Form and Content in the Proclamation of the Prophet Jeremiah*. BST 4. Zürich: EVZ-Verlag, 1970.

Biddle, M. *A Redaction History of Jeremiah 2:1-4:2*. AThANT 77. Zürich: TVZ, 1990.

Blank, S. *Jeremiah: Man and Prophet*. Cincinatti: Hebrew Union College Press, 1961.

Bright, J. *Jeremiah: Introduction, Translation, and Notes*. AB 21. Garden City NY: Doubleday, 1965.

Capra, F. *The Tao of Physics*. Third edition. Boston: Shambhala, 1991.

_____. *The Turning Point*. New York: Simon & Schuster, 1982.

Capra, F., D. Steindl-Rast, and T. Matus. *Belonging to the Universe: Explorations on the Frontiers of Science and Spirituality*. San Francisco: Harper, 1991.

Carroll, R. *Jeremiah: A Commentary*. OTL. London: SCM, 1986.

Craigie, P., et al. *Jeremiah 1-25*. WBC 26. Dallas: Word, 1991.

Cornill, C. *Das Buch Jeremia*. Leipzig: Chr. Herm. Tauchnitz, 1905.

Darr, K. *Isaiah's Vision and the Family of God*, Literary Currents in Biblical Interpretation. Louisville: Westminster/John Knox Press, 1994.

Diamond, A. R. *The Confessions of Jeremiah in Context: Scenes of Prophetic Drama*. JSOTSup 45. Sheffield: JSOT Press, 1987.

Dobbs-Allsup, F. *Weep, O Daughter of Zion: A Study of the City-Lament Genre in the Hebrew Bible*. Rome: Pontifical Biblical Institute Press, 1993.

Duhm, B. *Das Buch Jeremia*. KHC 11. Tübingen: J.C.B. Mohr, 1901.

Galambush, J. *Jerusalem in the Book of Ezekiel: The City as Yahweh's Wife*. SBLDS 130. Atlanta: Scholars Press, 1992.

Goldman, Y. *Prophétie et royauté au retour de l'exil: Les origines littéraires de la forme massorétique du livre de Jérémie*. OBO 118. Göttingen: Vandenhoeck & Ruprecht, 1992.

Heisenberg, W. *Physics and Philosophy*. New York: Harper & Row, 1962.

Herntrich, V. *Jeremia: Der Prophet und sein Volk: Eine Einführung in die Botschaft des Jeremia*. Gütersloh, 1938.

Herrmann, S. *Die prophetischen Heilserwartungen im Alten Testament: Ursprung und Gestaltwandel*. BWANT 85. Stuttgart: Kohlhammer, 1965.

_____. *Jeremia: Der Prophet und das Buch*. EdF 271. Darmstadt: Wissenschaftliche Buchgesellschaft, 1990.

Holladay, W. *The Architecture of Jeremiah 1-20*. London: Associated University Press, 1976.

_____. *Jeremiah 1: A Commentary on the Book of the Prophet Jeremiah Chapters 1-25*. Hermeneia. Philadelphia: Fortress, 1986.

Hubmann, F. *Untersuchungen zu de Konfessionen: Jer 11:18-12:6 und Jer 15:10-21*. FB 30. Echter: Echter, 1978.

Ittmann, N. *Die Konfessionen Jeremias: Ihre Bedeutung für die Verkündigung des Propheten*. Neukirchen-Vluyn: Neukirchener, 1981.

Janzen, J. *Studies in the Text of Jeremiah*. HSM 6. Cambridge MA: Harvard University Press, 1973.

Kuhn, T. *The Structure of Scientific Revolutions*. Chicago: University of Chicago Press, 1962.

Liwak, R. *Der Prophet und die Geschichte: eine literar-historische Untersuchung zum Jeremiabuch*. BWANT 121. Stuttgart: Kohlhammer, 1987.

Lundbom, J. *Jeremiah: A Study in Ancient Hebrew Rhetoric*. SBLDS 18. Missoula MT: Scholars Press, 1975.

_____. *The Early Career of the Prophet Jeremiah*. Lewiston NY: Edwin Mellen, 1993.

McConville, J. *Judgment and Promise: An Interpretation of the Book of Jeremiah*. Winona Lake: Eisenbrauns, 1993.

McKane, M. *A Critical and Exegetical Commentary on Jeremiah*. Vol. 1. *Introduction and Commentary on Jeremiah I-XXV*. ICC. Edinburgh: T.&.T. Clark, 1986.

Mowinckel, S. *Zur Komposition des Buches Jeremia*. Videnskapsselskapets skrifter 4, Hist.-Filos. Klasse, 1913 no. 5. Oslo: Kristiana, 1914.

Nicholson, E. *Preaching to the Exiles: A Study of the Prose Tradition in the Book of Jeremiah*. Oxford: Basil Blackwell, 1970.

Nogalski, J. *Redactional Processes in the Book of the Twelve*. BZAW 218. New York: Walter de Gruyter, 1993.

O'Connor, K. *The Confessions of Jeremiah: Their Interpretation and Role in Chapters 1-25*. SBLDS 94. Atlanta: Scholars Press, 1988.

Pohlmann, K.-F. *Studien zum Jeremiabuch: Ein Beitrag zur Frage nach der Entstehung des Jeremiabuches*. FRLANT 118. Göttingen: Vandenhoeck & Ruprecht, 1978.

_____. *Die Ferne Gottes - Studien zum Jeremiabuch: Beiträge zu den "Konfessionen" im Jeremiabuch und ein Versuch zur Frage nach den Anfängen der Jeremiatradition*. BZAW 179. New York: Walter de Gruyter, 1989.

Polk, T. *The Prophetic Persona: Jeremiah and the Language of the Self,* JSOTSup 32. Sheffield: JSOT, 1984.

Rad, G. von. *Wisdom in Israel*. Nashville: Abindgon, 1972.

Raitt, T. *A Theology of Exile: Judgment/Deliverance in Jeremiah and Ezekiel*. Philadelphia: Fortress, 1977.

Reventlow, H. *Liturgie und prophetisches Ich bei Jeremia*. Gütersloh: Gerd Mohn, 1963.

Rudolph, W. *Jeremia*. HAT 1/12. Tübingen: J.C.B. Mohr, 1947, ^{3}1967.

Seybold, K. *Der Prophet Jeremia: Leben und Werk*. Urban-Taschenbücher 416. Stuttgart: Kohlhammer, 1993.

Skinner, J. *Prophecy & Religion: Studies in the Life of Jeremiah*. Cambridge: University Press, 1922.

Smith, M. *The Laments of Jeremiah and Their Contexts: A Literary and Redactional Study of Jeremiah 11-20*. SBLMS 42. Atlanta: Scholars Press, 1990.

Steck, O. H. *Israel und das gewaltsame Geschick der Propheten: Untersuchungen zur Überlieferung des deuteronomistischen Geschichtsbildes im Alten Testament, Spätjudentum und Urchristentum*. WMANT 23. Neukirchen: Neukirchener, 1967.

Thiel, W. *Die deuteronomistische Redaktion von Jeremia 1-25*. WMANT 41. Neukirchen: Neukirchener, 1973.

Thompson, J. *The Book of Jeremiah*. NICOT. Grand Rapids MI: Eerdmans, 1980.

Turner, M. "Daughter Zion: Lament and Restoration." Dissertation, Emory University, 1992.

Unterman, J. *From Repentance to Redemption: Jeremiah's Thought in Transition*. Sheffield: JSOT Press, 1987.

Volz, P. *Der Prophet Jeremia*. KAT 10. Leipzig: A. Deichertsche Verlagsbuchhandlung, 1920.

Weippert, H. *Die Prosareden des Jeremiabuches*. BZAW 132. New York: de Gruyter, 1973.

Weiser, A. *Das Buch der Propheten Jeremia: Kapitel 1-25:13*. Fifth edition. ATD 20. Göttingen: Vandenhoeck & Ruprecht, 1966.

Articles and Essays

Albertz, R. "Jer 2-6 und die Frühzeitverkündigung Jeremias," *ZAW* 94 (1982): 20-47.

Balentine, S. "The Prophet as Intercessor: A Reassessment," *JBL* 103 (1984): 161-173.

Bogaert, P.-M. "Urtext, texte court et relecture: Jérémie XXXIII 14-26 TM et se préparations," *SVT* 43 (1991): 236-47.

Böhler, D. "Geschlechterdifferenz und Landbesitz: Strukturuntersuchungen zu Jer 2,2-4,2," in *Jeremia und die "deuteronomistische Bewegung*," ed. W. Gross, 91-127. BBB 98. Weinheim: Beltz Athenäum, 1995.

Biddle, M. "The Literary Frame Surrounding Jeremiah 30:1–33:26," *ZAW* 100 (1988): 409-413.

_____. "The Figure of Lady Jerusalem: Identification, Deification and Personification of Cities in the Ancient Near East" in *The Canon in Comparative Perspective*, 173-94. Scripture in Context 4. B. Batto, W. Hallo, and L. Younger, eds. Lewiston NY: Edwin Mellen Press, 1991.

_____. "Lady Zion's Alter Egos: Isaiah 47:1-15 and 57:6-13 as Structural Counterparts," in *New Visions of the Book of Isaiah*. JSOTSup. R. Melugin and M. Sweeney, eds. Sheffield: JSOT, forthcoming.

Bright, J. "Jeremiah's Complaints: Liturgy, or Expressions of Person Distress?" in *Proclamation and Presence: Old Testament Essays in Honor of Gwynne Henton Davies*, 189-214. J. Durham and J. Porter, eds. London: SCM, 1970; corr. ed. Macon GA: Mercer University Press, 1983.

Clines, D. and D. Gunn. "Form, Occasion and Redaction in Jeremiah 20," *ZAW* 988 (1976): 390-403.

Diamond, A. "Jeremiah's Confessions in the LXX and MT: A Witness to Developing Canonical Function," *VT* 60 (1990): 33-50.

Gerstenberger, E. "Jeremiah's Complaints: Observations on Jer. 15:10-21," *JBL* 82 (1963): 393-408.

Gunneweg, A. "Konfession oder Interpretation im Jeremiabuch," *ZTK* 67 (1970): 395-416.

Holladay, W. " 'On Every High Hill and Under Every Green Tree'," *VT* 11 (1961): 170-76.

Horst, F. "Die Anfänge des Propheten Jeremia," *ZAW* 41 [1923]: 94-153.

Jeppesen, K. "Mother Zion, Father Servant: A Reading of Isaiah 49-55," in *Of Prophets' Visions and the Wisdom of Sages: Essays in Honour of R. Norman*

Whybray on His Seventieth Birthday. JSOTSup 162. H. McKay and D. Clines, eds. Sheffield, 1993.

Jobling, D. "The Quest of the Historical Jeremiah: Hermeneutical Implications of Recent Literature," in *A Prophet to the Nations: Essays in Jeremiah Studies*, ed. L. Perdue and B. Kovacs, 285-97. Winona Lake: Eisenbrauns, 1984. (= *Union Seminary Quarterly Review* 34 [1978]: 3-12).

Kumaki, F. K. "A New Look at Jer 4,19-22 and 10,19-21," AJBI 8 (1982): 112-122.

Levin, C. "Noch einmal: Die Anfänge des Propheten Jeremia," *VT* 31 (1981): 428-440.

Parunak, H. Van Dyke. "Some Discourse Functions of Prophetic Quotation Formulas in Jeremiah," in *Biblical Hebrew and Discourse Linguistics*, ed. R. Bergen, 489-519. Dallas: Summer Institute of Linguistics, 1994.

Ruprecht, E. "Ist die Berufung Jeremias 'im Jünglingsalter' und seine 'Frühverkündigung' eine theologische Konstruktion der deuteronomistischen Redaktion des Jeremiabuches?" in *Schöpfung und Befreiung: Für Claus Westermann zum 80. Geburtstag*, ed. R. Albertz, et al, 79-103. Stuttgart: Calwer Verlag, 1989.

Seidl, T. "Jeremias Tempelrede: Polemik gegen die joschijanische Reform? Die Paralleltraditionen Jer 7 und 26 auf ihre Effizienz für das Deuteronomismusproblem in Jeremia befragt," in *Jeremia und die "deuteronomistische Bewegung*, ed. W. Gross, 141-79. BBB 98. Weinheim: Beltz Athenäum, 1995.

Seitz, C. "The Prophet Moses and the Canonical Shape of Jeremiah," *ZAW* 101 (1989): 3-27.

_____. "Isaiah 1-66: Making Sense of the Whole," in *Reading and Preaching the Book of Isaiah*, ed. C. Seitz, 105-26. Philadelphia: Fortress Press, 1988.

Smith, M. "Jeremiah IX 9—A Divine Lament," *VT* 37 [1987]: 97-99.

Willey, P. "The Servant of YHWH and Daughter Zion: Alternating Visions of YHWH's Community," SBLSP 1995 (forthcoming).

Willis, J. "Dialogue Between Prophet and Audience as a Rhetorical Device in the Book of Jeremiah," *JSOT* 33 (1985): 63-82.

Woudstra, M. "A Prophet to the Nations: Reflections on Jeremiah's Call to the Prophetic Office," *VR* 18 (1972): 1-13.

Zulick, M. "The Agon of Jeremiah: On the Dialogic Invention of Prophetic Ethos," *The Quarterly Journal of Speech* 78 (1992): 125-48.

Author Index

Polyphony and Symphony in Prophetic Literature.
Rereading Jeremiah 7–20.
by Mark E. Biddle.   Studies in Old Testament Interpretation (SOTI) 2.

Mercer University Press, Macon, Georgia 31210-3960.
Isbn 0-86554-503-0. MUP/H394.
Text and cover design, composition, and layout by Edd Rowell.
Camera-ready pages composed on a Gateway 2000
    (via WordPerfect 5.1/5.2) and printed on a LaserMaster 1000.
Text font: TimesNewRomanPS 11/13 and 10/12.
    Titles: Helvetica. Hebrew: ATECH. Greek: ATECH.
Printed and bound by Braun-Brumfield Inc., Ann Arbor, Michigan 48106
    Via offset lithography on 55# Natural Hi-Bulk paper.
    Smyth sewn and cased in .088 binder boards,
        rounded and backed, and with matching headbands.
    Cloth: Roxite C 56548 (blue) vellum finish,
        one hit on spine and c. 4 with gold foil S19.
    Dust jacket: 80# Rainbow Antique (blue-gray)
        printed PMS 539 (dark blue) (endleaves match dust jacket).
    Individually shrinkwrapped and packed in convenient cartons.
                                                    [March 1996]